The Travellers' Handbook

A Guide to the law affecting Gypsies

by
Bill Forrester

An InterChange Book

First published in 1985 by
InterChange Books, 15 Wilkin Street, London NW5 3NG.

© Bill Forrester 1985.

ISBN 0-948309-00-8

Copies from the publisher, payment with order, plus £0.60 P+P.
Trade distribution in the UK by:
  Turnaround, 27 Horsell Road, London N5 1XL.
  Scottish & Northern, 18 Granby Row, Manchester M1 3GE.
  Scottish & Northern, 48a Hamilton Place, Edinburgh EH3 5AX.

Forrester, Bill
  The Travellers' Handbook: a Guide to the law
  affecting Gypsies.
  1. Wayfaring life——Law and legislation——
  England
  I. Title
  344.202'87   KD4095

Cover photograph: The BBC Hulton Picture Library.
Cover design by Graham Betts.
Typeset by Cylinder Typesetting Limited,
        85a Marchmont Street, London WC1 1AL.
  Printed by Robert Hartnoll (1985) Limited,
        Bodmin, Cornwall.

Contents

Acknowledgements

The views in this Handbook are my own, but I must thank Ken Golding, who has the unenviable task of managing me; Bill Lane, Mike Lewis, John Grimwood, Jonathan Brown, Douglas Hayton, Colin Ismay, Graham Cheek, Wendy Hewing and Dot Smith for all the support and guidance they have given me in Essex, along with the many other officers, site wardens and managers, who help to deal with the problems of site-finding, and problems flowing from lack of sites. A particular tribute is necessary to the Chairman of the Gypsy Sites Working Group and the Social Services Committee, Mrs Joan Martin and Mr Frederick Thornton, Vice-chairman. Mrs Martin has visited numerous site locations, visited Travellers on some of the worst encampments, and has had to face the wrath of the public at meetings and through the post for nearly nine years.

I would also like to thank all those people who have helped me write this Handbook. They know who they are, but they include Diana Allen, Hughie Smith, Tom Lee, Penny Vinson, Elsie Fisher, Thomas Acton, Joan Collins, Richard Whiting, Geoffrey Bindman, Tess Richards, Jim Parish, Jocelyn and Graham Aldous, Stephen Sedley, Peter Kingshill, Lady Plowden, Anne Bagehot, Kit Sampson, Cecily Taylor, Mary Dixon, Donald Kenrick and Pam Lutgen, fomerly of the Department of the Environment Gypsy Sites Branch, as well as other personnel there; Brian Foster, Patricia Bell and others at the Greater London Council; and Don Buckland at the Department of Education and Science in Tunbridge Wells. Last – and she would never allow herself to be least – I want to thank Jill Barrett for her help and guidance during its latter stages.

The Handbook is dedicated to the memory of Don Byrne.

Bill Forrester

InterChange Books would like to acknowledge the financial assistance of the Greater London Council, the Joseph Rowntree Charitable Trust and the Minority Rights Group.

Author's Note

During publication of this Handbook, there was an important legal decision in the High Court. It particularly affects Chapter 5 (pages 27 to 49).

The case was brought by two individual Travellers against Hertfordshire County Council. They alleged

a. that it was in breach of its duty to provide pitches for gypsy caravans; and
b. that the Secretary of State for the Environment had improperly failed to exercise his powers of direction to secure correction of the county council's failure.

The Travellers asked the court for a number of legal remedies, including orders to direct Hertfordshire and the Secretary of State to properly carry out their duties and powers.

On 14 January 1985 the Judge, Justice Mann, decided in favour of the Travellers and granted a declaration. He agreed with the Ward case (see page 40) in saying that the Travellers had the right to bring the case (as 'gypsies' affected), and said that the Secretary of State's powers to decide when a local authority had not done its duty did not prevent the court dealing with the case.

The most important part of the judgement says that:

> In my judgement, the correct approach is to ask simply whether at the moment the question is to be answered, there is adequate accommodation for gypsies residing in or resorting to the area. If the answer is no, then whether the breach of duty should be visited by relief is a matter of discretion. So simple an approach seems to me appropriate, having regard to the language of the statute and to the consideration that the court is not dealing with a mere technicality but with the ability of people to have a secure accommodation for their homes (as presumably Parliament intended) and with the removal of the often grossly injurious environmental impact upon the public and local residents of unauthorised gypsy encampments.

No appeal has been lodged against the judgement in R v. Secretary of State for the Environment and Another *ex parte* William Lee, and the *Times* report of 15 January 1985 should presently be superseded by a fuller report in the Law Reports.

Introduction

This Handbook began its life one wet November weekend in 1975, at a National Council for Civil Liberties Groups' Meeting in Chippenham, Wiltshire. One day of that weekend was devoted mainly to Travellers, and those attending it included the late Don Byrne, then Adviser to the Minister for the Environment on Gypsy Encampments, representatives from the National Gypsy Council, and various other organisations. My most vivid recollection of that weekend was the showing of a short piece of film of a brutal West Midlands' eviction. This had been obtained by solicitors defending a Traveller charged with police assault. It showed unnecessary violence, the use of bulldozers, and children witnessing everything from a nearby fence. At the end of the showing, there was total silence in the hall.

Many such evictions have happened since then. How many? It is impossible to say. Pressures, complaints, the police, antisocial behaviour by Travellers, deaths, illnesses, weddings, better work elsewhere: all play their part in causing families to move on. Most movements are, fortunately, not by violent eviction. But that is no reason for complacency.

My involvement with Travellers began in Manchester and Salford in 1973. Twelve years on, Salford still has no site, and Manchester was 'designated' for years with a closed site. The facts speak for themselves. Since no-one wants Travellers, they cease to belong anywhere, then are criticised for not living neatly and cleanly without any proper facilities.

Since 1980 I have been Gypsy Liaison Officer with Essex County Council. In common with every other county council and local authority in the country, we have wrestled long and hard with the conflicting pressures of eliminating nuisances from unofficial encampments, while not harassing Travellers pointlessly from place to place, aiming both to get sites set up while not acting against the interests of the electorate who may imagine that an official site will be a disaster. My own experience of all but one of our seven Essex local authority sites, and all of the many private sites set up by or for Travellers, suggests that official sites can and must be established, and can and must be managed well.

This Handbook is a description and guide to the main laws and practices which particularly affect Travellers, relating to England and Wales, although there are some bibliographical references to publications on Scotland, Northern Ireland and Eire. They are *our* laws and practices. We, through our Houses of Parliament, elected Members of Parliament and central and local government machinery and institutions, have invented the legislation and distributed its powers and duties as we have considered appropriate. The Traveller community has played a minimal part in the process, and yet is bound by its results. Travellers can either accept being turned off their land by planning enforcement action, while the local authority for the area gets away with not providing the sites which it has a legal duty to provide, or they can withdraw co-operation and try to evade or defy the laws we have drawn up.

It is no longer a capital offence, as it was in Henry VIII's time, to be an 'Egyptian', but the operation of our laws and practices reflects attitudes and presumptions about them which are often at best unfortunate, regularly negative and sometimes overtly racist. I am convinced that sheer ignorance and lack of thought and experience is the biggest reason for the worst attitudes and prejudice. But this can be turned around. In Essex, I have recently been impressed by the careful and enlightened approaches of the parish councils, and the Essex Association of Local Councils, as well as the Country Landowners Association and the National Farmers Union. The answers, and this is the key point, lie with the settled population. The inescapable facts of life for Travellers in England and Wales are these:

1. The Caravan Sites Act 1968 has been in force for fourteen years. It has failed to produce the solution its creators planned. Only about half the country's Traveller caravans are on legal sites at any one time.
2. Roadside Travellers are moved from place to place, for reasons which may or may not be their fault. They are denied facilities and blamed for all resulting problems. Without security of tenure, many Travellers do nothing to help their acceptance, and mess and scrap thus become the most noticeable feature of their encampments.
3. Those who live and work near unauthorised, unplanned and often unsuitable encampments may well be forced to put up with undesirable

and unpredictable goings-on. The groups of caravan families on such sites are rarely managed, nor their numbers limited. They are just tolerated or suffered, and moved on when numbers, protests, problems, or a combination of these reach a certain level. But the movings-on reflect only frustration. They solve nothing, merely relieving another group of local people of the immediate problems which are caused by lack of planning and the provision of proper sites.

4. Many local authorities (and I would except Essex from this) only operate negatively towards Travellers. Positive planning policies and the determination to win solutions would make an enormous difference in overcoming the site shortages. Support for Travellers relieving the public purse by setting up their own sites in suitable places could be a crucial part of such a strategy, especially in rural areas. Travellers who lose that battle for planning, on an apparently suitable site, are far more embittered than if they had made no effort at all. Yet they face criticism if they do nothing to help themselves.

It should not be a question of whose side one is on, but of commonsense, good practice and firm, principled, informed political will.

1. Who is a Traveller?

The most important facts to remember, when discussing who is, and who is not a Traveller or Gypsy, is that about 9,000 caravans, which local authorities regard as 'Gypsy' caravans, have been recorded every six months since July 1978. Only half of these have been recorded on proper legal sites. Each of them contains a family or part of a family, and the chances are that those not on a legal site do not have one to go to. It is these facts which present the basic practical accommodation problem which must be solved.

There are lots of arguments about whether a group of caravan-dwellers comprise 'Gypsies' or 'tinkers' or 'didicois', or some other derogatory term, but those who engage in such arguments rarely explain what the benefit of the argument is. Are 'tinkers' not to be provided with sites? If not, what is to happen to them?

Serious arguments about the history and origins of Travellers are rather different. Sociologists, historians and anthropologists have studied their movements through different countries at different times. Judith Okely, in her recent book *The Traveller-Gypsies* (Cambridge University Press, 1983) provides an excellent review of many of these discussions. But the motives of scholars are often rather different from those of someone who wishes to prevent a site being built by proving that those living locally in caravans and travelling around are not Travellers. Such people and their arguments should be dealt with carefully and sceptically.

Section 16 of the Caravan Sites Act 1968 defines Gypsies as

> . . . persons of nomadic habit of life, whatever their race or origin, but does not include members of an organised group of travelling showmen, or persons engaged in travelling circuses, travelling together as such.

This is the definition which decides which groups local authorities must provide sites for, and who would be affected by 'designation' (site provision and designation are both covered in Chapter 5). The definition does not necessarily apply more widely, but is the only one in an Act of Parliament, so a future court in, for example, a Race Relations Act case would be likely to look closely at it if it had to decide on a definition for other purposes.

It should be noted that the Act's definition is by lifestyle, and not cultural, national or ethnic origins. It is based closely on the 1967 High Court definition in the case *Mills v Cooper*. In this, the Judge pointed out that someone could be a 'gipsy' one day, but not the next, as it depended on how 'nomadic' they were.

It is obvious that there must be some practical commonsense in dealing with the definition. If all those who settled on sites ceased to be Gypsies or Travellers, then they would all have to move off again – quite ridiculous.

Long periods of settlement do create difficulties, though. A Buckinghamshire Magistrates Court in 1972 decided that Thomas Frankham, cousin of Gypsy Johnny Frankham, the boxer, had ceased to be a 'gypsy' by being settled on his land for eleven years. Eton Rural District Council had said that it would not take action against Thomas if the court ruled he was a 'gypsy'. By contrast, a Chelmsford planning appeal in 1982, decided that a man named Adams *was* a 'gypsy', in spite of his being settled on his own land for at least ten years.

The Department of the Environment Circular 28/77 has this comment about Section 16 of the 1968 Act:

> This definition makes no distinction between different groups of Travellers or their trades. It includes romanies, didicois, mumpers, tinkers, hawkers etc . . . In law, therefore, the term 'gypsy' refers to a class of persons and is not confined to an ethnic group . . . The criterion 'nomadic habit of life' leads to a certain ambiguity, especially in relation to gypsies who settle for lengthy periods on authorised sites.

At about the same time, the Department commissioned the Cripps Report, which quoted the 1975 publication *Gypsies and Government Policy in England*, based on major research of the early 1970s:

> . . . if a group of Gypsies or Travellers recognises as a member a person calling himself a Gypsy, then his identity as a Gypsy is a social fact.

Cripps commented that: most of the gypsy officers employed by local authorities appeared to act on [the above test and that these officers] were not inconvenienced in practice by a lack of precision in the statutory definition [in Section 16].Cripps had no improvement to suggest.

Two other detailed definitions from other parts of the British Isles which they use for 'their' Traveller populations, are as follows: The Secretary of State's Advisory Committee on Scotland's Travelling People writes:

> People known variously as travellers, tinkers or gypsies, or by related names who, *by choice*, live in caravans, tents or other unconventional structures and . . . are *mostly nomadic* for all or part of the year. Covering a range of economic levels, they rarely take a regular employed job but make a living by a variety of work, partly seasonal, by collecting and dealing in waste materials, dealing in other commodities and by other forms of small scale self employment such as tarmac laying, fence painting etc. They are, by choice, generally socially separated from the settled community, and have been descended directly from travellers – i.e. they have at least one traveller parent – regard themselves as travellers and are accepted as such by the other members of the community.

The Travelling People Review Body in the Republic of Ireland defined Travellers as:

> an identifiable group of people, identified both by themselves and by other members of the community (referred to for convenience as the 'settled community') as people with their own distinctive lifestyle, traditionally of a nomadic nature, but not now habitual wanderers. They have needs, wants and values, which are different in some ways from those of the settled community. More than half of those in the group [this relates specifically to the Irish Republic] now have a place to live, either in houses or on serviced sites. Some may take to the road either occasionally or seasonally. The majority of those not yet provided with accommodation desire a fixed place of abode, and many of them are, in fact, encamped in locations with reasonable permanence. However, there are still a number of transient families.

In the absence of any better definition, that is perhaps where we should let the subject rest, while adding that many Gypsies prefer the description Traveller, which not only neatly covers a wide group, but does not have the same stigma that 'Gypsy' can have attached to it. This is the term we shall largely use in this Handbook, although as Gypsy (gypsy) is the term most often used legally, when discussing duties of site provision, for instance, that will be used. 'Gypsy' was coined from 'Egyptian' in the Middle Ages to describe Romany families. 'Gipsy' is a bastardised version of this, and not used in this book.

References

Mills v Cooper, 1967 (2), *All England Law Reports* 100.
B Adams *et al. Gypsies and Government Policy in England,* Heinemann, 1975.
Planning Exchange Forum Report 19: *Scotland's Travelling People,* 2nd report, Spring 1980, from the Planning Exchange, 186 Bath Street, Glasgow G24 HG.

2. Types of site

The land that a Traveller parks a caravan on decides which laws and property interests are affected, and who has the power to do something about it. A Traveller on his own land, for example, cannot be evicted by quick court action, but a Traveller on someone's else's land can almost always be turned off within a short time by the landowner, through court action, or even without any court order. A Traveller legally on a site run by a private person or a local authority has some protection from being evicted, and cannot be evicted by force, without a court order. Although this Handbook covers the particular legal position of Travellers, it is useful to note that the legal position of all caravan-dwellers is practically identical.

So let us begin with the ownership of the land. If the Traveller owns it himself, then he should have the deeds or some other good evidence of ownership, which should be kept very safe, as they are important documents. If he owns it, he will then be obliged to get planning permission for any 'development' on the land, and this will need permission under the various Town and Country Planning Acts, Regulations and General Development Orders. The important thing to remember is that any caravan in which a Traveller is living is likely to need planning permission. The sole exceptions are in the First Schedule to the Caravan Sites and Control of Development Act 1960, which says that you don't need permission for a caravan parked next to a house you are living in, or for up to 2 nights' stopping on land by a single caravan, up to a maximum 28 nights in any 12 months; or for up to 28 nights in any 12 months for up to 3 caravans, on at least 5 acres of open land with a single occupier; or – and this is an important exception for Travellers – for parking a caravan on land occupied by someone for whom you are doing seasonal agricultural or forestry work. There are a few other exceptions, including one for travelling showmen's winter quarters, but those listed are the most important for Traveller families. The First Schedule to the 1960 Act says that a site licence is not required for these exceptional circumstances; then the current General Development Order, which deals with national policy on planning and gets updated every few years, says that if a licence isn't needed, nor is planning permission.

If a Traveller owns the land and needs planning permission, or needs to persuade the owner of the land to try and get it, or to support the getting of it, then this Handbook will explain how to go about it. To find out what happens, or can happen, if a Traveller needs planning permission but doesn't apply for it, turn to Chapter 3.

If you are a Traveller on a piece of land with no arrangement with the owner, it is always worth trying to make some, even if you may not want to draw attention to the fact that you are there. If the owner is a large company or public body, they may not even be aware you are there for some time, or not want the bother of doing anything about it, unless and until they get complaints about your being there, however inaccurate, from people who live nearby. Don't forget, though, that a landowner without planning permission for a caravan site is unlikely to want an official arrangement with caravan-dwellers on his land, cannot take rent officially, but may be quite happy for a Traveller to be there, even if he protects his own position by serving a letter or notice on you to say you have got to move off. If no problems are caused to him or his neighbours, if waste is disposed of carefully and other Travellers are also there, doing the same, you are much more likely to get a long stop somewhere. In my experience, virtually all evictions (except where the land is needed for something else quickly) are prompted by complaints, and there are many Travellers who don't get complained about or moved on.

You may be on a piece of land and not know who the owner is. Some Travellers seem to have the gift of finding land where the owner is totally unknown. In England, unless a landowner is selling it, he or she can keep quiet about ownership of land. If a group of Travellers occupies land, the chances are that a landowner will issue a letter, or get a solicitor to do it, telling the occupiers to move off. But the land may be highway land (a roadside verge, former road or verge, or a lay-by) in which case it will be up to the local authority that is the highway authority to decide what happens. Or the land-owner may just not do anything. If that happens, it's as well to ask around the local area to find out who owns the land. It is just possible that it could be used as a proper site, so, if you have the money and wish to set up your own site, turn to Chapter 3 for advice on how to go about it.

Finally, you may be amongst the 4,000 or so Traveller families on a site that has proper planning permission, one run either by a local authority, another Traveller or private person or organisation, or your own site. If you are on a legal site, then you are free of the worries of being suddenly evicted by a landowner or fined for obstructing the highway, even if you have to observe site rules or your neighbours annoy you.

Almost half the 8,000 Traveller families in England and Wales have a legal place to stop. Since July 1978, in the middle of January and the middle of July each year, almost every district council and London borough has counted the Traveller caravans which are then parked on each type of site in its area. Some authorities count more often than that. These figures are then collected and published and analysed by the Department of the Environment's Gypsy Sites Branch, which operates from the Department's Eastern Regional Office near Earl's Court, London. When studying these figures, it is important to remember that they are a record of caravans, not pitch numbers, so that there may be 26 caravans on a 20-pitch site during January, and 15 caravans on the same site in July, while families are away, perhaps fruit-picking. While it is encouraging to see that the percentage of families on legal sites is rising slowly but steadily, it is still worth remembering just how many Traveller families will have to spend nights on dangerous stretches of highway verge, or with the threat of a dawn eviction from someone else's land.

References

Caravan Sites and Control of Development Act 1960, HMSO.
Town and Country Planning General Development Order 1977-83, HMSO.

Counts of Gypsy Caravans in England, each January and July since July 1978, from Gypsy Sites Branch, Department of the Environment, Charles House, 375 Kensington High St, London W14 8QH, phone (01) 603 3444 (See also analysis of figures to July 1982).
Sites provided by Local Authorities in England, also from Gypsy Sites Branch, address above.

3. Up against the planners

The single biggest obstacle to the proper provision of adequate Traveller caravan sites in England and Wales, from a technical point of view, is the planning system. Public protest and opposition to the setting up of sites may be considerable, but it only manages to stop them being built because of planning as it now exists.

Planning policies in Britain simply do not cater for Traveller sites. Purely residental caravan sites are hard enough to establish, but Traveller sites are well-nigh impossible.

Planning in this country is a mixture of law and policy. The Town and Country Planning Act 1947 is usually regarded as the starting point for planning law, and there have been several major planning Acts since, usually replacing the previous ones. The present major Acts are the Town and Country Planning Act 1971 and the Local Government Planning and Land Act 1980.

Although central government lays down the law and certain policy guidelines in General Development Orders (latest 1977-83), and has responsibility for motorways, the major trunk road network and certain other major works, such as nuclear power stations, it is local authorities who deal with day-to-day planning matters. There are appeals to the Minister of the Environment when a planning applicant disagrees with a decision of a planning authority. Traveller sites are usually dealt with by district councils, for private sites, or by district and county councils together, for local authority sites. In London, each borough deals with all cases.

Each planning authority has a legal duty to draw up outline plans for its own area. These used to be called Development Plans, but are now divided into Structure Plans (for each county) and Local Plans (for each district); each London borough has a Borough Plan. All such plans have to be finally approved by the Secretary of State for the Environment before they can be fully relied on by that authority or anyone else, and many of them contain nothing at all about Traveller sites. Nevertheless, as we shall see later, each county and London borough has a duty to provide sites, while the Secretary of State for the Environment has the power to enforce this. He doesn't, however, use this power, even in blatant cases, so it seems that local authority planning departments can ignore their legal duty with impunity.

It is hardly surprising, therefore, that Traveller sites are both difficult to establish and to get planning permission for! In towns, if land is expensive, land with planning permission is even more so and planners do not like caravans between houses, nor industrial areas near residential ones. And Traveller sites tend to be both industrial and residential.

In country areas, much land is green belt, and planners don't like 'ribbon development' or 'sporadic development' or 'consolidation of sporadic development'. Areas of 'outstanding natural beauty' or 'special scientific interest', too, seem to be regarded as incompatible with caravans. It would appear that unless a Traveller family has been in a place many years (probably on their own land, or that of a brave, friendly landowner) or are in the middle of nowhere surrounded by trees or hedges or a wall, getting planning permission is going to be a struggle.

By 1980, the majority of privately-owned legal Traveller sites round London was in the Metropolitan Green Belt, reflecting a lack of proper planning policy, but demonstrating also that exceptions to it are sometimes made. In 1977, John Cripps, in the report of his nine-month survey commissioned by the Department of the Environment, *Accommodation for Gypsies*, commented:

> Generally, permission for a site for caravans of any kind is difficult to obtain in an isolated position owing to restrictions on sporadic development; and there has long been a virtual ban on them in green belt and equivalent areas. The servicing of isolated sites is also costly, often to the point at which it cannot be entertained.

He continued:

> Planning authorities, however, are least inclined to permit a house to be built, or a caravan stationed, on the relatively isolated site which Gypsies prefer and may even be obliged to occupy.

The biggest headache for the planners seems to be the fact that Travellers are almost always self-employed, living and working from the same place, adding up to 'mixed use' in planning jargon. In other words, if you live in a caravan, the planners find it hard to find a place for you, but if you deal in scrap next to your caravan, planners have no corner for you, officially. The result tends to be that everyone tends to turn a blind eye to scrap-dealing or other business in order to get a site past a planning committee.

It is clear that there must be planning, and that there must be planning enforcement to prevent people doing what they like in unsuitable places, Travellers no less than others.

But Traveller sites must be included in future plans, not because of Traveller numbers, tiny compared with those of the rest of the population, nor because of the area of land they need, which is also tiny, but because the problem of where sites go is far greater than numbers or size would suggest. They must at least have a fighting chance of getting planning permission, instead of it being all fighting and precious little chance.

Buying the land

Many Travellers buy pieces of land without advice, without proper legal searches, and sometimes merely by exchanging cash for title deeds. That means they have a piece of land, but it may be one on which they have little chance of ever getting planning permission for their caravan.

Before buying, it is always a good idea to get advice on the chance of getting planning permission. It is not necessary to ask the local planning department what the chances are, or even to notify them, although their advice will be free. You can go to a planning consultant who is sometimes part of an estate agency business, or to a surveyor or solicitor for confidential advice. They will charge, but it could save a great deal in the long run. If you decide to buy, the next question concerns:

Moving onto the land

This question is an important one. It is a choice that only a Traveller is likely to have to make: that between staying on the roadside and moving onto a piece of land which does not yet have planning permission for a caravan.

The risks are prosecution for running a caravan site without a licence, and/or an enforcement notice under the planning acts, instructing the site owner to remove the caravan within a certain time.

The advantage of moving onto the land is that it can help later if the land is developed as a good-looking site which fits into the area well, so that an inspector from a later planning inquiry might be impressed when he visits. Moving reinforces the argument that the Traveller owner has nowhere else legal to go. But it is very important that moving onto land is either linked to a planning application, or at least a fight against enforcement proceedings.

It seems ironic that Travellers who commit the planning 'infringement' of living on land without planning permission should be in no worse a position than a family which remains elsewhere while permission is being decided on. But, as a Department of the Environment Inspector said at a inquiry I recently attended, 'A planning inquiry is not a criminal trial. The question is whether the development should be allowed here or not. The Traveller is not being tried for moving there without permission.' In this particular case, the family had moved from a local authority site pitch to their own piece of land; they lost the appeal and are still fighting. But such cases are rare. Most Travellers have a choice between a roadside encampment, or some other land which they do not own, and their own piece of land. In my experience, most Travellers in this position move onto their own land.

The most important thing to remember is that if you move onto a piece of land without planning permission, it is unwise, and often very expensive, to ignore planning enforcement action and hope it goes away. That may work for a while, but once you have seen, as I have, someone fined £1,000 for staying on their own land, you think again. In another case in my experience, a landowner divided his (or her, the ownership remains unknown) land into 70 plots, which were sold, and re-sold, for between £600 and £3,000. Seven enforcement notices were served in early 1982. Three people from the thirty or forty who were on the land at any one time appeared at the appeal, represented by a property developer who knew little about the subject of Traveller sites. The appeal decision made a big issue out of the ownership of the land, which should be irrelevant for planning purposes, and quoted out-of-date figures for the number of Travellers in the district. The inspector decided, therefore, that there was no great need for a further site in the district, and that there was no good reason to allow that particular green belt site to have planning permission. The site occupants ignored the three-month period allowed by the inspector and were prosecuted for failing to observe an enforcement notice. They did not attend the first court hearing, and have now elected to be tried at the Crown Court. But it may be too late for them.

Planning permission

If you have a spare piece of land and have moved on to it, but are not sure whether to try to get a caravan site permission for it, then you can delay.

The advantage of applying for planning permission is that there is a chance, dependent on the attitudes of the local council planning committee members to Travellers, and the location of the piece of land, that the local council will grant planning permission for the site. It may be a small chance, but it is worth taking for it could save you much time, worry and money. If it is granted, you would not then need to appeal.

The disadvantage of applying immediately for planning permission is that it draws attention to your site – although unless you are in the back of beyond, you will of course have been seen already. A more important disadvantage, however, is that it speeds up the process. I came across a case recently where someone had been spending each summer on the same piece of land, without permission. As it was not 5 clear acres, he would not have been allowed 28 days there, let alone several months. But no planning officer visited him until a resident in the next village complained.

The ideal situation occurs when the planning authority takes some time to decide what to do, and you put your planning application in just before they decide, which they then do in your favour. But this is very unlikely. The best course is to get early advice from a planner or solicitor. If you choose not to do that, or cannot easily afford it, then make an early decision about applying for planning permission, talk to people who visit you from the planning department, and get them to help you to fill in any forms which you find difficult, especially any which they demand you fill in. Once you have decided to apply, let the planning department know immediately. Don't let them put you off, for example, by telling you that your application will be refused.

Caravan or bungalow?

Some Travellers would only ever wish to live in a trailer, but others like the idea of a more permanently-based dwelling, like a mobile home, bungalow (with or without caravan alongside) or house. The decision usually depends on money, but it is worth thinking ahead about which you would prefer, and even putting in alternative planning applications for (say) a bungalow and a caravan site. Don't forget that you rarely have to begin using planning permission as soon as you get it. Outline permissions, for the general idea of what you want to do, without the exact details of its design, usually last five years, and full permissions, which include exact details as well, often mean you only have to start building within three years. Obviously, if you want to live in a caravan on the land for some years before you build a bungalow, then you will need permission to keep the caravan there, as well as build the bungalow, but it is worth finding out early on if you can get permission for the bungalow. I know of at least one case where the planning appeal decision allowed the caravan to remain as living accommodation while the bungalow was built, as long as it was started within a specified number of years. Perhaps someone should try applying for permission to do just that, if that is what they want to do.

It is difficult, and probably not wise, however, for me to try to give advice here about specific instances. The best advice in any case is always to go to a qualified planner, surveyor or solicitor who is interested in caravan sites, knows something about them and Travellers, and who knows also about local planning policies and practice in the area where you are applying. You will have to pay, unless you are very lucky indeed! But it will give you the best chance of winning a legal place to stay.

Applying for planning permission

There is not enough space in this Handbook to cover the fine detail of making a planning application. But any adviser, or your local district or London borough planning department officers, will be able to explain what details you have to include on the application form, and which forms you have to send to other people who own interests in your land, if any, or live nearby.

Don't forget you have to pay a fee for a planning application, which is index-liked to inflation. It costs £47 until 31 March 1985 for an outline planning application for 0.1 of a hectare, or part of that, or a full planning application for the erection of 'each dwelling unit'. In case you are thinking of saving money by not applying, I am afraid you also have to pay for planning appeals if you haven't paid a fee for an application. So you finish up paying the same fee, except that, the longer you delay, the more likely the cost is to go up, because it is index-linked to inflation.

Once you have put your application in to the district council or borough planning department, they have eight weeks to decide whether to grant permission or refuse it. If they want more time, they have to ask you to agree. If you don't, or they don't contact you, then you can treat this as a refusal, and go for an appeal if you wish. But if you are not on the land, or you change address, don't forget to keep in touch with them so that they know where you are, or give them a fixed address of a friend or relative, on a legal site, or in a house.

During the eight weeks, the district council planning department should hear from the people you or they have sent forms to, and who will say if they object to your application. The parish council will also be consulted. This is the time when you really need friends – and find out who they are! It is vital that your neighbours are reassured that you will be a good neighbour to them, that you don't make noise late at night, have dogs which attack the local cats, or children who wander onto property and attract suspicion if anything goes missing. It is much more difficult for a Traveller to get support from a traditional community if the Traveller is an unknown quantity, but many have done so, and it has been of invaluable help if neighbours don't object to their planning application, and if the parish council for the area does not object either. The latter, simply by not objecting, is giving tacit support. That can be vital when planning committee councillors are considering whether to grant planning permission, especially when planning policies for an area do not, as few do, include Traveller caravan sites.

If you are granted planning permission, and you are happy with any conditions put on it (such as, for example, that it is limited to a few years, to yourself and your family, so that you can't sell it on to someone else; or that it requires you to plant trees round it or do other works), then you can skip the next section and go on to that on site licences.

Refusal

You or your adviser will get a Notice of Refusal if the planning committee turns your application down. Unless you decide to give up (perhaps because your adviser says you can never win on that particular piece of land, although such advice would be rare), you then have six months to appeal against the refusal. The notice you have got will say why the planning committee say they have turned it down (the 'grounds for refusal'), and that will be the starting point for your appeal case.

Once you decide to appeal, you then have two more choices. One is: how soon shall I do it? The best advice on this is probably: once you have decided to do so, go ahead with it. If you are living in your caravan on the piece of land itself, then the local authority can serve an enforcement notice on you as soon as they turn your application down. Many planning authorities do not, but they can prod you into action by doing so.

The second choice is: do I want a public inquiry? Opinion is divided on this. My own opinion is that this is always a good idea, because it gives everyone (Traveller appellant, planning authority, county council officers, local residents, local councillors or anyone else who feels they might be affected by the site) the chance to express their views publicly, and (even more important) everyone can ask everyone else direct questions. But other Gypsy Liaison Officers argue that they have won more appeals through what are called 'written representations'. Every appellant can ask for a public inquiry, or can agree to the appeal being settled by an exchange of letters between the inspector, the planning department and themselves. The choice is the appellant's, however, and that is important: it's up to you.

Whichever method of appeal you choose, it's important that you work hard with your adviser to put over the best case you can. You should definitely have a skilled (probably qualified) adviser by this stage, who can tell you your best arguments under the various sections of the Town and Country Planning Act 1971, which covers grounds for appeal against enforcement notices and planning refusals. That is not the whole story, however, because your adviser will also be drawing the inspector's attention to government circulars. These are advisory policy notes to local planning authorities, not legally binding, but something which the planning authority should always 'consider'. They are issued mainly by the Department of the Environment, and its Gypsy Sites Branch in its Eastern Regional Office; this is also the department which has a Planning Inspectorate employing the inspector who decides your appeal. As well as explaining circulars, your adviser will be explaining the local position of Travellers in the area (are there legal sites? how many? where?), and your own personal circumstances, and past history (have you always been a Traveller? if not, for how long on the road? where?). Your adviser may also refer to government publications, for example, the 1977 Cripps Report; figures from the counts of Traveller caravans conducted by every district council in mid-January and mid-July since July 1978; and may in addition call on a representative of the county council to talk about plans for further, or any, local authority sites in the county, surrounding districts and especially the district containing your land.

The public inquiry, if you decide to have one, is likely to be held in the district council building, and is much more friendly and less formal than a court case. The inspector will welcome everyone, explain what the appeal is all about, and then the appellant, your adviser or representative or yourself, will explain why you should be granted planning permission. The council will explain why you should not be given it, and each side will call its witnesses. You are likely to be called to give details of your past history which may help show you have nowhere else to go, while the council will call its planning officer. Then your side will have the final word.

An inspector will visit your site, either alone or with your representative and the council's, or sometimes both, during or before or after the inquiry. He will then go away for some months, usually, although it may be quicker, until you get your written decision. If you lose the appeal, you are likely to get a few months' grace, at the end of which you must have moved off. The length of that time may be, but quite often is not, based on the amount of time you have been on the land. Sometimes you will be expected to move to a local authority site pitch that has been 'held' for you, but in my experience it is rare for this to happen, and rarer still that a family fighting for a private site would be happy on a local authority site. This should ideally be a subsidised benefit, and only for those who cannot afford their own land.

Established use

No section on site planning would be complete without a mention of what is called Established Use. This falls between full planning permission and enforcement action. The brief details are as follows.

When the Town and Country Planning Acts 1947 and 1962 were passed they made it necessary for people to get planning permission for land use which previously had not required such permission.

The Town and Country Planning Act 1971 says that if someone began using land before the beginning of 1964 without planning permission and has used it continuously for that purpose since the end of 1963; or if they have used it with planning permission granted before the end of 1964, but with conditions attached to it which they have ignored since the end of 1963; or in one other instance not likely to be important for Travellers, then any person 'having an interest in the land' (owner, long-term tenant etc.) may apply for an Established Use Certificate under Section 94 of the Act. This certificate is not a planning permission in itself, but it prevents the local authority taking, or, at least, winning enforcement proceedings against a Traveller.

It makes little difference, in theory, if you apply for a certificate or wait until the planning authority takes action against you, if they do. In many cases of long-term stopping, they won't. In practice, it does make a difference. If you can prove continuous whole or part-year (say, during the summer) stopping by caravans, without planning permission, since late 1963 or earlier, then go for a certificate. Not only will it prevent your having to prove it all later, when your witnesses may have moved, or even died, or their memories of 1963 become blurred and vague, but it should also prevent the planning authority taking any enforcement action against you. There is no point in waiting for legal action against you, if you can avoid it, but your proof of the matters in Section 94 must be strong. Trying to get a certificate and failing could obviously be worse than not trying at all.

Note that the use by caravans need not be by the same person or people, but it must be continuous. Note also that you must have an 'interest in the land' to apply for a certificate. That means you must own the land, or be a tenant or licensee of it, not just squatting on it.

References

Town and Country Planning Act 1971, HMSO.
Town and Country Planning General Development Order 1977-83, HMSO.
Local Government Planning and Land Act 1980, HMSO.

Department of the Environment booklets on planning applications, appeals and public inquiries, available from the Department, 2 Marsham St, London SW1, phone (01) 212 3434. Department of the Environment Circular 24/73 (on assessment of viability of smallholdings), HMSO.

R.J.F. Gordon, *Caravans and the Law,* Shaw and Sons, 1984, (Bell Green Lane, London SE26, phone (01) 659 5432.)

—— , *Law Relating to Mobile Homes and Caravans*, Shaw and Sons, 1984.

R. Home, 'Planning Problems of Self-help Gypsy Sites', *Journal of Planning and Environmental Law*, 1982, p. 217.

Public Inquiries Action Guide, from Community Action, 27 Clerkenwell Close, London EC1, phone (01) 251 3008.

Planning appeal decisions are not binding on other inspectors. They are not published, but some are covered by other publications like the *Journal of Planning and Environmental Law*. Actual decisions can be obtained from the planning authorities involved, the Traveller Appellant (or the adviser/ solicitor involved) or the Department of the Environment Planning Inspectorate, Tollgate House, Houlton St, Bristol BS2 9DJ, phone (0272) 218811, quoting the appeal reference (begins 'APP/') if at all possible.

Local planning help may be available from planners through the Planning Aid Unit of the Town and Country Planning Association, 17 Carlton House Terrace, London SW1Y 5AS, phone (01) 930 8903.

4. Licensing, site design and management

The obtaining of planning permission tends to be the biggest obstacle to overcome in setting up a private or public Traveller site, but it is not the only hurdle that a local authority or a private site operator has to overcome to make sure of a satisfactory and successful site.

Site licences, site design and site management are linked to planning permission because every site has to have them, to begin with; they are linked to one another because each site licence has to be compatible with the planning permission, and the licence (and any conditions attached to it) may well influence the design of the site. A well-designed site will of course be much easier to manage than a badly-designed one. For the commercial operator as well as the local authority site operator, careful design is also much more likely to lead to cheaper running costs, meaning higher profits or better savings.

Just because licensing, design and management follow planning permission, it doesn't necessarily mean they should not be planned for in advance. The private commercial operator will be concerned with all three; the single-family site owner will be concerned with the first two; the local authority will not, as we shall see, need to bother with a site licence, but will be concerned with the second and third.

Licensing

The requirement for a site licence is additional to the need to have planning permission, and has a different purpose, but the planning permission and site licence must 'hang together' so that they do not contradict one another. The same basic law that applies to all others applies to Travellers. The most important piece of legislation is the Caravan Sites and Control of Development Act 1960, which introduced local authority controls over all caravan sites, invented site licences, and gave local authorities the wide powers they needed to set up and run caravan sites.

The subject of licensing is fully covered for lawyers and others professionally interested by *Caravans and the Law* by R.J.F. Gordon, (Shaw and Sons, 1984), so I will not go into great detail here.

All private and company site operators, including Travellers and their families setting up their own sites, must get site licences for any site they are running which operates all the year round, and for most part-year sites, too. Local authorities are the only operators who do not have to get a site licence for their own sites. District councils and London borough councils actually issue site licences, usually through, or at least with the guidance of, their Environmental Health Departments, so it would be daft if they had to issue one to themselves. County councils used to have to get a site licence from the district for all caravan sites they were running on their own land, but since Section 176 of the Local Government, Planning and Land Act 1980 was passed, county councils can run Traveller sites on their own land without needing a licence. This is one of the rare cases where the law is different for Traveller sites.

If a caravan site is temporary *and* is one of the types of site listed in the First Schedule to the Caravan Sites and Control of Development Act 1960, (near the end of the Act) then, as noted earlier, no site licence is needed. The most useful of these sites to Travellers, unless they own a house with a caravan next to it, are likely to be those offering the chance of stopping one or two nights on a piece of land under 5 acres (maximum 28 nights in a year); over 5 acres, up to 3 caravans for up to 28 nights in any year; and, particularly, the right to stop on a farm while doing 'seasonal work' for the farmer, of which too few farmers (and often too few Travellers) take full advantage. As farm work gets scarcer, with high unemployment and advances of mechanisation, many farmers pay lower rates, and Travellers on a highway verge 'play the market' between farmers in the area who need potatoes lifted or fruit picked. The Act's other exceptions are not likely to be so useful to Travellers.

Unless the person applying has held a site licence which has been revoked within the three years before his application, the district council or London borough council has to grant a licence to anyone granted planning permission. This may have been given by the district council or on appeal, but it must be a full permission, not just an Established Use Certificate (described in Chapter 3). The site licence must be granted for the same length of time as the planning permission.

Section 5 (1) of the 1960 Act lays down, however, that the local authority which must grant the site licence can attach conditions, where it thinks it 'necessary or desirable . . . in the interests of (1) persons dwelling on the land in caravans (2) any other class of persons and (3) the public at large'.

The individual Traveller site owner may well have limited money available for its development. He is unlikely to be able to get any grants towards building or other costs. He certainly will not be entitled to any of the government funds that local authorities can use for their site design and total buildings costs. Unlike those building or buying houses, he is only likely to be able to get a mortgage from a building society or bank with several years' proof of income (even though the land and site could be sold over his head if he failed to keep up the payments, or left the site and disappeared). Local authorities are not able to grant conventional mortgages for caravan sites (the legislation specifies 'dwelling-houses'), but under Section 3 of the Local Authorities (Land) Act 1963, as amended by Section 43 of the Local Government (Miscellaneous Provisions) Act 1982, a local authority may advance money (secured by a mortgage) to any person to enable him to acquire land, or carry out building work on it, where the authority is satisfied that it would be for the benefit or improvement of its area to do so. If an authority can be satisfied, firstly, that it will get its money back from the Traveller, secondly that an authorised site in an appropriate place is a 'benefit or improvement of its area' and, thirdly that it will bring that district nearer to Designation under the 1968 Act (see Chapter 5) then it would be most worthwhile to explore the possibility of getting such a mortgage. However, as far as I know, no such mortgage has yet been granted for a family Traveller site.

The individual site owner will have to stick to the planning permission and site-licence conditions when designing his site or having it designed for him. He will also be subject to building regulations, and have to negotiate with the water authority, the electricity board and so on, over the provision of services. It is obviously outside the limits of this Handbook (as well as the expertise of its author!) to suggest specimen designs, but it is probably a good idea to have a look at Department of the Environment Circulars (especially DoE 28/77, which includes site layout plans), as well as *Gypsy Sites Design Guide*, published by the Department in 1979, for ideas.

The private commercial site operator will have the same limitations of planning permission conditions (if any), site licence conditions (if any) and building regulations to abide by, but may well not be in the same difficult financial position. For such an operator, it is likely to be a question of whether the site will be a profitable enterprise, not whether it will be a better alternative than a roadside verge.

Section 5 of the Act specifies the sorts of conditions which may be attached relating to numbers of caravans allowed; positioning; site screening; fire prevention, detection and equipment for fighting it; and 'securing and maintaining adequate sanitary and other facilities, services and equipment'.

This last was obviously considered important by Lord Justice Danckwerts. In the 1963 case, Chertsey Urban District Council v Mixnam's Properties, in the Court of Appeal, he stated that the purpose of site licence conditions was to secure:

> the provision of proper facilities in respect of sanitation and amenities so that the site should not become a menace to the health of the occupants of the caravans or other persons who might be affected by the site, and also to prevent the site becoming an eyesore, or in any other way a nuisance to the members of the public who may dwell in the neighbourhood or pass through the locality.

Section 5(6) of the 1960 Act refers to 'model standards' which may be specified by the Secretary of State for the Environment, and which local authorities are directed to 'have regard to' when deciding if and what conditions should be attached to a site licence. But as far as Traveller sites are concerned, Department of the Environment Circular 28/77, published in March 1977 just prior to the Cripps Report, stated in paragraph 7 that 'The model standards prescribed under section 5(6) . . . are not appropriate for gypsy caravan sites and should not stand in the way of greater flexibility in the type of provision.'

A site owner may appeal against site licence conditions within twenty-eight days of the issue of the licence. The site owner appeals to the Magistrates Court for the site's area. There is no right of appeal for a caravan dweller who is not the site owner. The test is whether the condition(s) appealed against are 'unduly burdensome', for example because they contravene the types of condition the local authority is allowed to impose on the site owner.

Site design

Let us consider site design for each of three types of site operator: the individual Traveller family site owner; the private commercial operator who is planning a site for occupation by Travellers and the local authority (county, district or London borough) which is providing a site under the Caravan Sites Acts 1960 (and perhaps 1968 as well).

Local authority site designers are in a rather different position from the others. They have to observe the terms of the planning permission, but it may well have been granted by their own colleagues' planning committee, and contain minimum conditions which reflect the confidence an authority should have in its own ability to run sites. There will be no need for a site licence for a Traveller site run by a local authority, and, as district councils have a duty to develop such sites under the 1968 Act, there will be no worry over building regulations unless the county council is designing and developing the site.

But local authorities have an extra limitation to offset their major financial benefit, compared with individual Travellers running family or commercial sites. The whole capital cost of building (and designing) a Traveller site provided under Section 24 of the Caravan Sites and Control of Development Act 1960 (incorporated into the 1968 Act) is met by central government, as long as the plans have full financial approval before building begins. The grant approval machinery works through the Regional Office of the Department of the Environment, with guidance from the Department's Gypsy Sites Branch. All final approvals are given by the relevant junior Minister, currently the Sports Minister, Neil MacFarlane.

Central funding came about in July 1978, following a major recommendation of the Cripps Report. Initially, funding was provided for under the Appropriation Acts, but it is now authorised under Section 70 of the Local Government, Planning and Land Act 1980.

The limitations on local authorities are, firstly, that site designs must satisfy DoE requirements, initially laid out in the 1979 *Gypsy Sites Design Guide*, though this has since been modified, and, secondly, that there are 'guideline' figures for the cost per pitch which different authorities can get from central funds for site building costs. Unless they have been able to establish a good reason (such as exceptionally high development costs, and no other possible better site in the area), the pitch figures since October 1979 have been:

£10,000 for permanent residential sites in rural counties; £11,000 in outer London; and £12,000 in Central London. Transit site pitch guideline figures are £5-7,000 per pitch. There is now some considerable flexibility upwards in these figures.

The standards which the Department requires have definitely led to an improvement in site design and site building quality. This in turn leads to easier, and often cheaper management and a much pleasanter environment and better standard of living for Traveller occupants, who have usually had previously to endure years of roadside encampments, without facilities, security of tenure or protection against harassment or sudden eviction.

Site management

The individual site owner will not have to concern himself with management and its problems. The private commercial operator will only have this worry if he employs staff to run the site, although he will have a duty to maintain it properly, collect rents and make sure no nuisance or damage is caused to neighbours, and, if it is, to deal with it.

The best study of local authority Traveller site management (*The Management of Local Authority Gypsy Sites*) was published by the Department of the Environment and the Welsh Office in 1982. It is a shortened version of a research report commissioned by the DoE, from Ian McGill of Brighton Polytechnic. It says, correctly, that applied commonsense is the best guide to good management, together with the flexibility to appreciate and understand that the Traveller lifestyle often differs from those of house-dwellers. It also points to the need to realise that different groupings of Traveller families may not mix with one another.

References

Caravan Sites and Control of Development Act 1960, HMSO.

Gypsy Sites Design Guide, update information from Department of the Environment Gypsy Sites Branch, address given in Chapter 1. I. McGill, *Management of Local Authority Gypsy Sites*, Department of the Environment, 1982 (full version available only in DoE Library).

Ministry of Housing and Local Government Circular 42/60. (This Ministry was the predecessor of the DoE.)

R.J.F. Gordon, *Caravans and the Law,* Shaw and Sons, 1984.

Chertsey Urban District Council v Mixnam's Properties, Court of Appeal, 1964 (2) *All-England Reports* 627.
Complaint against Wandsworth London Borough, Investigation 438/S/79, Commission for Local Administration; also Complaint on Luton Borough Council, Investigation 171/H/77. Address at end of Chapter 5.

Third Report, Session 1979-80, Parliamentary Commissioner for Administration, HMSO (concerns Hartlebury Site, Worcestershire).

Quality of Site Provision, National Gypsy Council Report, 1976, from NGC, Greengate St, Oldham, Greater Manchester, phone (061) 665 1924.

5. Local authority sites: provision and designation

Local authorities are wonderful creations. They have lots of different departments, all of them having different duties to carry out. They even have different divisions of duties, depending on where they are, which may also determine the size. Counties include many district councils within their boundaries, and the Greater London Council includes all London boroughs. In London, the GLC is responsible for waste disposal, the fire service and strategic planning, but not waste collection or social services; each London borough deals with housing, social services, and many other matters. In the six metropolitan counties such as Tyne and Wear around Newcastle, Merseyside around Liverpool, Greater Manchester, West Yorkshire around Leeds, South Yorkshire around Sheffield, and the West Midlands around Birmingham, all facing abolition in 1986 with the GLC, there is a similar division, except that the GLC no longer controls transport. It does control education in inner London, through the ILEA; the metropolitan counties have no education function. But in the rest of the country, the 'shire' counties, as they are called, each county council deals with social services, some planning matters, education and highways etc., while each district council deals with housing, environmental health and much else.

As well as being confusing, these do not always work well all the time in all places. But there is some method in the apparent madness, and there should always be helpful people along the way to tell you that it's the district council you want, when you've traipsed all the way to the county council offices!

The present system has been operating since April 1974. It is important, when trying to understand Traveller site provision, to remember that the duty to provide sites, and, before that, the power to do so, was there before the 1974 changes. And a few decisions from before 1974 are still important.

We have already seen how the planning system does not usually allow for Traveller sites. We have also seen that local authorities don't have to worry about site licences, and that they can reclaim site building costs from central government.

The Caravan Sites and Control of Development Act 1960 powers of site provision, together with local authority reorganisation, mean that all local authorities (counties, districts/boroughs and London boroughs), apart from the City of London and the Greater London Council, have wide powers to set up and run caravan sites, including Traveller caravan sites, under subsection 4 of section 24 of the 1960 Act. They include the provision of facilities, acquiring land, and (subject to limitations like not being able to provide caravans, and having to make 'reasonable charges' for use of sites, services or facilities provided by them), 'a local authority shall have power to do anything appearing to them desirable in connection with the provision of such sites'. Of particular interest is subsection 4 of the Act, which makes it possible for a local authority to 'make available the services and facilities provided under this section for those who do not normally reside in the area of the local authority as freely as for those who do'.

The Caravan Sites Act 1968

The combination in the 1960 Act of site provision powers, site licence controls and powers to close sites down was not good news for the many Traveller families who lived in makeshift sites on spare pieces of land. Although accurate figures are hard to come by, it seems that more sites were closed down than were set up. Certain local authorities, for example in Kent and Hertfordshire, did set up some caravan sites, but these were only enough for a tiny number of families to live on. The lack of progress with site provision in the 1960s led to increasing pressure for a legal duty of site provision, including pressure from the Gypsy Council (formed in 1966), the National Council for Civil Liberties and the Association of Public Health Inspectors.

The Liberal MP Eric Lubbock (now Lord Avebury) was already planning a Bill to protect caravan site residents from quick eviction or harassment when the Labour government asked him, in 1968, to add a second part to it, on Traveller site provision. After all-party support in Parliament, and major changes, including making it a duty for each London borough and metropolitan county borough (now metropolitan county) to provide a limited number of caravan pitches, the Bill finally became the Caravan Sites Act 1968.

Broadly, what the Act does is put an unlimited duty on shire counties, and a limited duty on each London borough and each metropolitan county for each of their districts, to provide caravan sites for 'gypsies' 'residing in or resorting to their area'. The only other limitation in the Act is that the duty to provide sites is 'so far as may be necessary', an expression not so far legally defined. Outside London, the county has the duty to decide what sites are needed, and to obtain the land (or switch from its own stock in other use); the district has the duty to develop and manage 'gypsy' sites in its area. In return for providing enough sites, the Minister 'designates' an area as having 'adequate accommodation' for 'gypsies'. It can be a London borough, a whole county, or an individual district or group of districts within a county. The local authorities which cover the area 'designated' can then take quick legal action to evict Travellers not on legal sites.

Let us look closely at the 1968 Act, and at what its effects should be, and have been. It has been altered by Section 190 of the Local Government Act 1972, because of local government reorganisation, and by certain sections of the Local Government Planning and Land Act 1980, mainly in regard to funds for site building and designation. But the original duty in Section 6 remains the same in its intention. The amended Section 6(1) says:

> Subject to the provisions of this and the next following section (7), it shall be the duty of every local authority being the council of a county or London borough to exercise their powers under Section 24 of the 1960 Act (provision of caravan sites) so far as may be necessary to provide adequate accommodation for gypsies residing in or resorting to their area.

That basic duty is then reduced for each London borough and for metropolitan counties in each of their districts by Section 6(2):

> The council of a Metropolitan County or London borough shall not in any case be required under subsection 1 (above) to provide accommodation for more than *fifteen* caravans at a time in each district in the county or, as the case may be, in the London borough.

Table 1 summarises the site provision duty:

Table 1: General duty: 'So far as may be necessary to provide adequate accommodation for gypsies residing in or resorting to their area'

Greater London boroughs	Metropolitan counties	Shire counties
Each borough can only be legally required (at most) to provide 15 caravan spaces on sites for Gypsies 'at a time'	Such a county can only be legally required (at most) to provide 15 Gypsy caravan spaces in each of its districts 'at a time' (These counties are threatened with abolition in 1986. Paragraph 18 Annex A of the white paper *Streamlining The Cities* says their site functions will be transferred to district councils.)	There is no legal limit to the number of Gypsy caravans such counties must provide for

Who and what decides the limit of the duty where it is unclear: the Minister for the Environment, using Section 9 of the 1968 Act or a 'designation' order.

Greater London

The Greater London Council, as noted earlier, has no duties or powers to provide caravan sites for anyone. Interestingly, the London County Council which preceded it until 1963 did have such powers. The Greater London Council did appoint two job-sharing workers in 1983, however, to 'liaise and outreach' to Travellers as part of its Ethnic Minorities Unit within the Director-General's Department.

As the GLC is not involved with site provision duties under the Act, each London borough has the duty under Section 6 to use the powers in Section 24 of the 1960 Act to set sites up, and to run them.

Outside London

The position is very different in the metropolitan and shire counties. You will remember that Section 6 begins by saying 'Subject to the provisions of . . . the next following section'. Section 7 of the Act 'splits' the duty of site provision in each county between the county and the district, and, arguably, creates a recipe for indefinite delay in site provision.

Section 7 says that the county council's duty 'shall extend only to determining what sites are to be provided and acquiring or appropriating the necessary land', so the county council must decide where the sites are going to go, but does not (except by special local agreement) build and run them. More importantly, the split duty means that the county and district council have to work together to get the site running, not necessarily the easiest of tasks where political control differs – or even where it doesn't!

Section 7 says that the district council's duty, when the site is located in its area, is 'to exercise all other powers under Section 24 [of the 1960 Act] in relation to the site'. So, legally, a district must build and run any site in its area which is provided by the county for Travellers under the 1968 Act, unless county and district vary by agreement, allowed for in Section 7(3). In practice, Section 7 has not produced such a sharp division of duties. The 1982 Department of the Environment booklet *Management of Local Authority Gypsy Sites*, based on a survey commissioned in 1979-80, found that eleven county councils (all shire) managed one or more sites themselves. No such information is easily available on site development, but in my own county of Essex, for example, the sites are all run by districts, even though the County Architect has designed and built all but one.

How Traveller caravan sites are set up

Sections 6, 7 and 8 of the 1968 Act may all play a part in the setting up of a site, so let us see how a typical site might be established. (It is as well to bear in mind that no site is really 'typical'.)

The suggestion for a site location may come from one of a number of sources. It may be county council land, which one department does not need any more, and thus declares surplus. It may be district council land in a similar position, perhaps where the district doesn't want a site in the place the county council has suggested. It may be privately-owned, with an owner keen to sell because he has been refused planning permission for what he wants to do on it. It may be a piece near where Travellers have stopped for many years, even centuries, where the owner is unwilling to sell, but where there is also no suitable county or district land nearby.

It is at this stage that political considerations almost invariably creep in. In my experience, not so much in Essex but in places such as Swansea and Inner London, the majority group on a district or county council will usually do its best to put a site in a minority member's ward or constituency. If the seat is marginal, reasons will be found to reject the site proposal, however good technical assessments may be. That does not mean that all sites finally finish up like this, but these practices are so widespread that technical officers should arguably begin with a political map of the area in order to prevent needless and costly investigation of proposed sites that are doomed from the start. The battle may, of course, be a long and fierce one: I know of at least one instance where control of the council changed part-way through, with the new council not only reversing the old one's support for a site, but putting in a rival bid to buy the land from another council controlled by the same party. The Minister for the Environment is now deciding if the site will go ahead.

London boroughs have these battles internally, but in the counties (where the whole residue of site provision duties rests: there is no fifteen-caravan limit outside London and the metropolitan counties) the position is complicated by several factors. Will a county fall out with a district over Traveller sites, for instance? Will that prevent co-operation on other matters? Will county councillors put up indefinitely with complaints about unofficial camps? Will districts let them?

The Section 6 duty is quite clear: county councils decide, and county councillors must therefore be bold and deal with the problem. District councils must be consulted over site proposals, under Section 8 of the Act, and they may object to the Minister for the Environment about a site which the county decides on against the district's wishes, but the county council should not be deterred from setting up a good site by veiled threats from a district. Any county councillor who believes that proper sites improve matters should welcome the long-term benefit of a better connection with a district where complaints about unauthorised Traveller camps disappear. Essex County Council has had two Section 8 objections to the Minister against sites within the last three years. Both have been rejected, and the first site is now running with the co-operation and help of the same parish council which fought it tooth and nail earlier.

Let us suppose that the county council selects a site which it doesn't own. Some shire county councils seek the view of parish councils, after getting district council agreement, or deciding to go ahead without it. Essex holds a public meeting, preceded by an exhibition on the site proposal. Councillors and officers from county or both councils discuss the proposal with all those who attend the meeting. Then, advised by county council officers, a working group of social services committee councillors decide at the next of their two-monthly meetings whether the social services committee should be recommended to pursue the site further.

If this is to be the case, the county planning committee (through its development control sub-committee) must decide whether to grant it planning permission or not. The various county councils put the responsibility for promoting Traveller sites onto different departments, but it tends to be placed under either the social services, chief executive's or (especially in the north of England) the planning department. Where the last has the responsibility for initiating and pursuing Traveller site proposals, it is then going to its own planning commitee for planning permission. Whoever the land belongs to, the county council can always grant itself permission for its own projects (or even proposed projects), although in the case of 'gypsy' sites, Section 8 of the 1968 Act requires the county council to consult the district before it decides to acquire any land for the site.

When the land for the proposed site is not owned by the county council, and the owner is not willing to sell, protracted discussions tend to take place, sometimes over a period of years, before the county council finally serves a compulsory purchase notice on the owner. Unless the notice persuades the owner to sell (which he can always do, to bring the procedure to an end), it starts off a chain of events which will almost invariably lead to a public inquiry. At that, the county council will have to prove an overwhelming need for the particular piece of land to be taken over and used as a Traveller caravan site. Objectors at the inquiry can include not only the landowner(s), who are known as 'statutory objectors', but also others who live in the vicinity or who have some other reason for claiming to be affected by the proposed site, the 'non-statutory objectors').

At such a public inquiry, the county council may be taken to task for rejecting other proposed sites for political reasons. But the Department of the Environment inspector who handles the inquiry is not likely to be concerned about the local politics of the area. He *is* rightly concerned about whether someone should have their land taken away from them, against their wishes, for a Traveller site. As has been said in several compulsory order cases, there must be a bona fide reason for the land to be compulsorily acquired, as someone's land is not to be lightly taken away from them.

After the inquiry – and it may be a long time after – the

Department of the Environment notifies the council of its decision, which may have been made by the inspector himself, an increasingly common occurrence, although Traveller site cases are often regarded as too politically charged for an inspector alone to decide. Alternatively, the decision is the Secretary of State's for the Environment. It is obviously a crushing blow to both the county and district councils if the compulsory purchase order is not confirmed. In Essex, all Traveller site plans for a district (or part of it) can be halted for three or four years while we negotiate with a landowner, perhaps fail to reach agreement, and then go through a long compulsory purchase order procedure, with all the requirements of the serving of notices, the exchanging of letters between lawyers for both sides and so on. It is an important and rigorous procedure with the proper safeguards, necessary in order to protect the rights of landowners. But it claims massive time and money, and any local authority deciding to put a Traveller site on land owned by an unwilling seller should think long and hard before doing so, examine the history of sites that have been rejected, and only proceed if it is a proper gamble with the ratepayers' money.

There is clear evidence that the same long compulsory purchase delays happen in other authorities. Hertfordshire has recently decided not to use the procedure for Traveller sites, while West Sussex (with Dorset, one of the only two counties which is 'designated' over its whole area) used a compulsory purchase order on only one of its thirteen sites.

Section 8 of the 1968 Act requires a county to consult a district where a site is proposed before going ahead and 'acquiring or appropriating' the land. 'Acquiring' refers to the county council buying new land; 'appropriating' means the council changing the use of land it already owns, to use as a Traveller site.

If the district council objects to the site, and the objection is 'not disposed of in consultation with the council of the county' (which is a very friendly way of describing what is often a not very friendly argument, probably whipped up by local press reports), then the district may object direct to the Minister. He deals with the matter usually through written exchanges with the county and the district, and then decides whether the proposed site is to go ahead or not. Section 8(3)(c) also allows him to direct the county to make an application for planning permission. The county council applies to itself for permission for its own Traveller sites, and the Section 8 objection to the Minister may only be made by the district after permission has been granted by the county planning committee. It is suggested that Section 8(3)(c) simply does not apply in such cases, and the Minister just decides whether to direct the county council to abandon or proceed with the proposal.

Exemption

Under Section 6(2) of the Caravan Sites Act 1968, it was possible until 1980 for a London borough or county borough to claim that it should not have any duty to provide Traveller caravan sites. In London, a borough had to prove that 'suitable land' was not available for a site in its area. Outside London, a county borough could use the same argument, or it could also get let off its duty if it could prove (to the satisfaction of the Minister) that between 2 May 1963 and 1 May 1968 'the number of gypsies resorting to the borough . . . was not such as to warrant the provision by the council of accommodation for them'.

The Minister's power to exempt was, in fact, only used in certain cases. No London boroughs were ever exempted. No local authority got exemption by proving it had no 'suitable land' (though many tried, and there was even a House of Commons debate on what that expression meant in London). Twenty-six county boroughs were exempted. All proved to the Minister that their gypsy population between 1963 and 1968 did not justify the provision of a site. All were exempted between 9 September 1970 and 5 March 1973. (They are listed in Appendix B of the Cripps Report.)

In 1974, county boroughs were abolished by local government reorganisation. But the exemptions continued in the former county borough area.

Paragraph 5.4 of the 1977 Cripps Report recommended:

The law to be amended to remove the Minister's power to grant exemption and to cancel all existing exemptions.

Section 173 of the Local Government, Planning and Land Act 1980 did exactly that, and the exemptions ended on 13 November 1981.

Exemptions are now part of history. But they are important, because they help explain the massive delays in site provision which have taken place in some areas. In Salford in 1973, for example, Salford Corporation claimed exemption due to lack of 'suitable land' in its area. It was turned down by the Minister. It then renewed its claim, while regularly evicting Travellers from derelict land in its area, using an injunction to prevent named families from stopping on *any* land owned by it! It never got exemption, but it delayed site provision by four years until the responsibility was taken over by Greater Manchester Metropolitan Council in April 1974.

Southend, Essex, was a county borough until April 1974. Exempted on 5 March 1973, it then lost exemption in November 1981. Since then, in the face of evidence from newspaper cuttings and from its own employees, it has persisted in arguing that no gypsy site is needed in Southend. It has not explained where it expects its local Traveller families to go.

Designation

Designation is a different matter altogether. It has often been described as 'the carrot', while the Minister's 'powers of direction' under Section 9 of the 1968 Act have been described as 'the stick'.

Designation was invented by the 1968 Act, and toughened up by the Local Government Act 1980, and most local authorities regard it as their reward for the provision of Traveller sites. Some even seem to regard it as something approaching Nirvana, usually when they don't as yet have a designation order!

The idea of designation is novel and simple, and nothing at all like it otherwise exists in English law. A local authority which has provided enough site provision for the 'gypsies' 'residing in or resorting to' its area gets a designation order for its area, approved by the Environment Minister and ratified by Parliament, which allows it to prosecute and/or evict Gypsy families who are not on legal sites in its area.

There are two unique aspects to designation, from a legal point of view. One is that the local authority can prosecute and/or evict Traveller families from land that the authority does not even own or control. All land, except where the landowner has given permission – when an authority would use planning laws against the owner, or prosecute him for running a caravan site without a licence – is included. The second unique aspect is that the local authority can go to the Magistrates' Court, which can grant an order which allows it to do its own eviction. Normally, the Magistrates Court does not deal with land cases at all.

Up until 1980, the original Sections 10, 11 and 12 of the 1968 Act meant that:

1. Only whole counties (or London boroughs) could be given designation. Dorset was the only county to be given it, in summer 1978.
2. Prosecution or eviction could only be of individual and named Travellers.

Now the position is different. Sections 174 and 175 of the Local Government, Planning and Land Act 1980 now mean that:

1. District councils (or groups of districts) can get designation orders, although they have to apply jointly with the support of their county council. The test is 'adequate accommodation' for Gypsies 'residing in or resorting to' the relevant area.
2. Once a designation order has been granted, a local authority in that area can evict a whole group of Traveller families in caravans by proving that just one caravan amongst them is not entitled to be on the encampment.

There is no doubt that designation has become increasingly important during the last few years, to Travellers and local councils alike. After the initial spate of designation orders between August 1972 and May 1975, during which time 13 London boroughs and 10 county boroughs got designation, there was a pause while Cripps reviewed site provision and reported, and then Dorset became the first whole county to get designation. Since that time, parts of Buckinghamshire, Kent, Wiltshire, Derbyshire and other counties have been designated, while West Sussex has become the second whole county to be granted an order.

Designation creates 'no-go' areas for Travellers who move in no particular pattern, but whose work prospects tend to take them all over the country. Designation is designed as the anti-Traveller powers reward for local authorities who have 'done their bit' over site provision. It does not guarantee that the area will be kept free of Travellers; the powers can only be used to evict and/or fine people who are camped in a particular place. The exercise of keeping an area clear of encampments could be expensive and ultimately pointless for the local authority. Most sensible authorities will only use designation powers against encampments where there are legitimate complaints. But the police may get involved in prosecutions in designated areas in a way that they would not in a non-designated area.

Designation orders can be granted by the Minister either when the authority has provided 'adequate accommodation' for Travellers who live in or resort to its area, or when the Minister considers that it is 'not necessary or expedient' for it to provide this. For there is a policy behind designation. As we have noted, no London borough has to provide more than fifteen caravan spaces under the 1968 Act. But this does not mean that fifteen-caravan sites are 'adequate accommodation' for its Travellers. The London boroughs of Westminster (1974) and Camden and Islington (both in 1981) were granted designation orders without providing a single site pitch. In Westminster's case, the evidence of Travellers was minimal or nonexistent, but both Camden and Islington consistently had Traveller families in their area, and Islington was found guilty of maladministration by the Local Ombudsman for trying to pretend that Travellers didn't camp in the borough.

Designation remains pernicious and probably unworkable. It will increasingly make movements by Travellers more likely to be illegal, as more areas become designated on inadequate figures which only include 'local' Travellers. If numbers rise steadily, then designation orders granted on one set of population figures will go out of date over time. Yet there is no evidence that such orders are ever revoked. Plymouth's order remained legally in force while its site was closed indefinitely, although the Department of the Environment sought assurances that it would not use its powers while the site was closed.

Designation, since it has been invented, is likely to be with us for the indefinite future. But would that all district councils were like Harlow in Essex, which could be granted an order, but which sees no need for one. If all Traveller families in an area were accommodated or tolerated, designation would be unnecessary.

Enforcing the site provision duty

The Minister for the Environment was given the powers of decision-making on Gypsy sites by the 1968 Act. Under this, the Minister is the only person who can decide if a local authority is or is not providing the sites it should be. If the authority has provided enough sites, the Minister, who decides what 'enough' is, grants a designation order. But if it has not done so, or not provided any sites, then what does he do?

The plain answer, ever since Section 9 of the 1968 Act came

into force on 1 April 1970, is nothing at all. Certainly, by 1979 the power to direct a local authority to provide had never even been threatened in writing against an authority. It is possible that either the London boroughs of Ealing or Hammersmith and Fulham, or even both, had Section 9(2) mentioned to them when they each planned to close down their long-established Traveller sites. In Ealing's case, it closed its site to return the land to Green Belt, but now is apparently selling the land to a property developer for £4½ million. But the Minister has never, under any political party, used the Section 9 powers of direction, or the power to enforce those directions by a writ of mandamus (which is used for directing authorities to do something) through the High Court. Eric Lubbock (Lord Avebury) was advised, when drafting the Bill in 1968, that it was standard practice to include such a power of direction, and that Public Health Acts, for instance, operated in this way.

During the years since 1968 we have seen a drift back to more local authority powers of decision-making, if recently set against rigorous central government proposals for centrally-controlled 'rate-capping'. Ministers' failure to use the Section 9 powers still sticks out like a sore thumb. Remember the Clay Cross Councillors who in the mid-1970s refused to implement the Housing Finance Act 1971, and who had their powers put into the hands of commissioners, with some councillors 'surcharged' and personally bankrupted? Remember Norwich Council in the early 1980s which refused to sell council houses, and which also had a commissioner from the Department of the Environment down to visit them, to 'speed up' council house sales? Both these councils, and they are only two examples, broke laws and had greater powers used against them.

In 1979, Michael Heseltine, when Environment Minister, proposed the abolition of many controls on local government, and the local government associations welcomed this with open arms. The Associations of County Councils, Metropolitan Authorities, District Councils and London Boroughs together published 1,000 controls they wanted to see lifted, which included lots of archaic Ministerial controls that were no longer necessary, but also many controls which standardised house-building quality and the like. Among the thousand proposed abolitions was Section 9 of the 1968 Act. Curiously, Section 9(2) was not abolished by the Local Government Planning and Land Act 1980, although the rest of the section was repealed. If this section had not been retained as a 'reserve power'

(as the DoE tend, diplomatically to call it), then of course any
Traveller might be able to take a county council or London borough
to court for not providing a site.

Section 9 has been discussed at least four times by a major
court. Although the 1967 High Court case of Mills v Cooper was
reported in the main law reports, the 1973 case, Kensington and
Chelsea London Borough Council v Wells, a Court of Appeal case
on the 1968 Act, was only reported in local government reports.
One would have thought it deserved a wider audience in the legal
profession.

The headnote to the report, which provides a résumé of the
decision, says that the Court of Appeal held that

> unless and until the machinery provided by Section 9 of the
> (1968) Act was invoked, the councils were not in breach of their
> statutory duties under Section 6; further, that, as a statutory
> remedy in respect of such breaches was given solely to the Minister,
> the court would not interfere, even though the statute gave no
> individual the right to make representations to the Minister, and
> would not, in any event, grant a mandatory injunction in such a
> case.

In other words, the Court of Appeal decided in 1973 that Section
9 gives the Minister power to force local authorities to provide
Traveller sites; because he must make a decision first that they have
not done their duty, no-one else (no court, usually) can make that
decision; and unless and until he decides to use that power, a local
authority is not failing in its duty to provide sites; further, the local
authority can evict Traveller families from its land without providing
them with a site, and no individual can enforce the site provision
duty.

On that last very important point, which does not appear in the
headnote to the case, Lord Justice Roskill said (at page 299) that the
duty to provide sites

> . . . does not . . . create in an individual living within the district a
> correlative personal or individual right to have that duty enforced
> for his own benefit and at his own behest against the local authority.

It all seems a very long way from the description of the 1968 Act as
the 'Gypsies' Charter', a term appearing in press reports in the late
1960s and early 1970s.

If the law had remained as the Court of Appeal interpreted it in 1973 in the Wells case, then the local authority duty of site provision would have remained unenforceable by Travellers.

Ten years later, however, the courts grappled again with the issue. On 7 February 1983, the High Court's Mr Justice McCullough dealt with R v the Secretary of State for Wales, an unsuccessful challenge to the Secretary of State's refusal to use his Section 9 powers. The Travellers had lost the first round. But in June 1983, the Traveller residents of the Westway site in Hammersmith, West London, were threatened with possible eviction. Unlike the occupants of the site in adjacent Ealing, the Westway residents took the matter to the High Court before Hammersmith's decision to abandon their connection with the site was implemented.

The site is owned by the GLC, and has been leased to Hammersmith since 1975. The running costs have been shared between Hammersmith and Kensington and Chelsea Boroughs since the site opened. Although it contains only 20 pitches, both boroughs got designation orders in exchange for providing it. Remembering the strict legal duty on each London borough council is site provision for 15 caravans at a time, perhaps the presumption in 1975 was that 30 caravans would occupy the 20 pitches?

Westway site is below the Holland Park Interchange on the M40 Westway which straddles much of West London. It is such a polluted and unhealthy spot that recorded lead levels in the blood of site children have sometimes been far in excess of limits considered safe. Prior to 1983, some of the families took successful High Court legal action which required Hammersmith to abate specific nuisances which threatened the occupants' health. Faced, too, with high running costs, Hammersmith responded by trying to hand the site back to the GLC, and abandon its connection with it. The Judge in the High Court case both commented that it was probably illegal for the GLC to run the site, and also that Hammersmith's suggestion that all it was doing was returning the site to its owners on the expiration of the tenancy was '. . . a wholly unrealistic description of what was happening. The Borough in truth and in fact was giving up its duty under Section 6 of the Act to provide a site.'

The full judgement in R v Secretary of State for the Environment *ex parte* Ward is an important one, for several reasons. And it has not gone to appeal:

1. It decided that an individual Traveller, though not able to

claim a personal caravan site place under the 1968 Act, may ask the High Court to set aside a decision by a local authority which had not properly done its duty under the Act.

2. It decided that the removal of the Minister's power of exemption in 1980 means that the Section 6 duty is now absolute. In Hammersmith's case, the extent of that duty was probably reinforced by the designation order which resulted from the Westway site. Closure of that site was therefore wrong, as Hammersmith had not taken into account its Section 6 duty, which continued.

3. The Judge said that he did not accept 'that a Designation Order under Section 12 [1968 Act], even on the ground that it is not expedient to make provision, puts an end to the duty of a Borough under Section 6'.

4. He also said that Section 9 covers neither the situation where the complaint is that there has been 'a failure of the Secretary of State himself to properly exercise his powers under the Act' nor where what is sought is 'a review of the manner in which the local authority has exercised its discretion'. He went on to say that 'irrespective of whether or not the Secretary of State would make a direction under Section 9, the local authority is still required by law to properly consider how it will exercise its discretion in respect of the duty placed upon it by Section 6 of the 1968 Act and the powers which it is given by Section 24 of the Act of 1960'.

5. The Judge concluded his judgement, however, by saying that: '. . . what is or is not 'adequate accommodation' is a question in the first instance for the authority concerned which has to make a value judgement taking into account all the circumstances' but this is also qualified by the fact that except in exceptional circumstances, the Court will not seek to enforce that duty but leave the matter to the Secretary of State 'who can be expected to only exercise his powers when it is appropriate to do so'.

With that final dry comment, we are left with an important landmark case, but it must be remembered that it is a High Court case (the Wells case was in the – superior – Court of Appeal), and that the Hammersmith case was dealing with an official site threatened with closure. It remains to be seen how a future court will deal with a similar case.

Preventing closure of one local authority site by long, complicated and expensive court action, however, does not mean more sites are provided. The biggest handicap to any improvement at present is the attitude of the Department of the Environment that local authorities should deal with their own problems, including Traveller site provision. That means that the Minister does not even investigate the reasons for site provision delays, let alone decide that the authority is not making a proper effort. Which authority will not produce lists of possible Traveller sites when pressed to do so? Which authority will not plead local pressure as a reason for the lack of sites? And yet county and London borough authorities have not only the site provision duty, but the power to override all unjustified opposition to provide sites on their own land, with only the risk of a Section 8 objection from the district.

The idea of the Minister not intervening in local authority affairs is not new, and not invented by the present government. In 1976, a House of Commons statement on Traveller site provision said that the use of Section 9 could upset the 'independence of local authorities'. It would seem, then, more important to allow local authorities to evade their legal duties under an Act of Parliament than to upset their independence. And yet Section 9(2) was retained in 1980. Could that have been to protect individual local authorities against a pile of legal cases from furious and dissatisfied Travellers whose patience had been exhausted by persistent moving on to avoid the same authorities which are breaking the site provision laws? Before you decide that this is a cynical view, consider if there could be any other reason for retaining it. The only authority that the present Minister would proceed against would be one which stated openly that it would not provide Traveller sites. Which authority would need to do that?

Commissioner for Local Administration (Ombudsman)

In contrast with court actions and political pressure, it is instructive to look at another method for trying to enforce the 1968 Act duties. The Local Ombudsman (or Commissioner for Local Administration, to give the present Dr Yardley – and previously Baroness Serota – their full title) can get behind the reasons for delay in site provision, and they publicise in their reports what they find out on the way.

What has not yet happened is any legal case based on an Ombudsman's decision as regards maladministration by a local authority.

The local Ombudsman system was set up when local government was reorganised in April 1974 following the Local Government Act 1972.

At least six complaints have so far been made to the Ombudsman over individual local authorities' failure to provide Traveller caravan sites. These have been against the London boroughs of Brent, Hackney, Islington and Tower Hamlets; the counties of Kent and Epsom in Surrey have had complaints outside London. There have been other such cases concerning Travellers, but not directly relating to failure to provide sites.

In London, where there is no duty to consult with other authorities, the complaints against Hackney, Islington and Tower Hamlets were all upheld. As stated, Islington was found to have effectively tried to deceive the Department of the Environment into thinking that no Travellers camped in the borough in 1975; the Ombudsman's decision was in August 1979. Islington's reward for its attempted deception, even after it proposed a Traveller site which was too expensive for the Department of the Environment to pay for, was a designation order, which has entitled it, since 1981, to boot out Travellers who camp in the borough; it has used this freely.

Hackney and Tower Hamlets were both found guilty of maladministration in 1977 for failing to provide a Traveller site. Hackney in 1983 still had no site, but Traveller families still camp where and when they can in the borough. Tower Hamlets finally opened a site in 1983, and is now aiming for designation.

The Brent case seemed to conclude by saying that it was not Brent that was at fault, but the Department of the Environment for failing to reply to a vital question which Brent had asked about designation in return for housing being provided for Traveller families.

The failures of the Kent and Epsom cases, and the relative success, from their point of view, of the London boroughs, underline the difficulties posed by two-tier local government, and the lack of enforcement powers against counties reluctant to upset their districts.

The 1977 Cripps Report recommended (at paragraph 4.43) that a 'quota' system should be introduced for each responsible authority, and that Section 9(2) should be used against an authority 'in the unlikely event of a local authority being unwilling to accept their quota and agree a programme'. Cripps suggested Section 9(2) should be used by the Minister to specify a period during which the authority must provide sites. This 'quota' system did not find much favour with central government, although figures are negotiated between local authorities and the DoE when designation is being discussed, and the Cripps recommendation fell largely on stony ground.

Sites and money

Since 1978, and now under Section 70 of the Local Government Planning and Land Act 1980, 100 per cent grants are available for the capital costs of designing and building Traveller caravan sites, to a local authority acting under the powers in Section 24 of the Caravan Sites and Control of Development Act 1960.

This means that if a proposed caravan site is approved by the Minister for the Environment for Section 70 grant, before any development begins, then the local authority which is building the site – be it county, district or London borough – gets back the whole agreed cost of

1. Land acquisition (or valuation, if it is already the authority's own land)
2. Design fees
3. Development to the approved standard

The Department of the Environment has guideline figures for the cost of both permanent residential and permanent transit Traveller sites; it also has a sites design guide. Both are modified in particular cases, so I am not including exact details of either. Local authority architects can directly contact their Regional Office of the Department of the Environment, for guidance. There is, however, some difference in guidance from such offices!

Although the whole cost of a site which has been financially approved is covered by central government, it is still counted as part of the local authority's 'capital expenditure'. Whatever county or district or London borough department is responsible for site provision, costs of site building fall within Block 5 ('Other Services') of the block grant controls invented by the Local Government Planning and Land Act 1980. This means that Traveller sites compete for priority in spending, with libraries, fire stations and the like.

There are two problems which tend to arise from this. One is that local authorities that are overspending according to central government on capital projects, annual ones that don't repeat, for instance, and long-term buildings, don't have any incentive to spend on Traveller sites. They did between 1979 and 1980, but the same Act which legalised grants for sites also put limits on local authority spending on them and everything else. The second problem is that all the things that can happen to delay or prevent sites being set up make it extremely difficult for any local authority to plan its spending on them. So that part of the Department of the Environment which deals with Traveller site grants and has to budget for them gets annoyed; the part of the DoE which deals with capital spending controls and block grant allocations also gets annoyed; and local treasurers and finance departments in local authorities get a bit annoyed too! If the reason is a delay in a decision from the Planning Inspectorate or over a compulsory purchase order, from yet another part of the Department of the Environment, the whole affair can become ridiculous; one part of the DoE asks the local authority what it is going to spend on a site which is held up by a delay in a decision by another part of its own department!

Management

Whoever is going to manage a site, planning for it should begin as soon as the site is definitely going ahead. If too early, ratepayers' money may be wasted on abortive work; if too late, delays may cause huge problems.

In London, each borough runs its own site(s), if it has any, and most, as mentioned, do. The only exception is the Westway site, currently under threat of closure, which is run by Hammersmith but co-funded by Kensington and Chelsea. Both were designated when it opened.

In counties, districts will normally run sites, with either the housing or environmental health departments responsible for them. The same is true in London, although almost all are run by housing departments. Where the county council is running the site, it will usually be through its social services department.

Section 7 of the 1968 Act requires the county council to repay the district council its losses on the running of sites 'reasonably incurred under this section'. For that reason, county councils fix rents on sites, and Gypsy Liaison Officers or others from the county council will keep an eye on spending by districts, and deal with advice on site management problems.

Some conclusions

The whole question of local authority site provision was examined by Cripps; two paragraphs of the 1977 Report are particularly relevant. His paragraph 3.19 reads:

> *The Pressure of Public Opinion.* The most obvious reason for the failure of local authorities to provide more sites is the pressure of public opinion. Dozens, even scores and sometimes hundreds of possible sites may be investigated and eventually eliminated without one being chosen, so determined are the opponents of each and every alternative. A councillor who fails to oppose a site in his ward immediately feels that his seat is in jeopardy. Courageous men and women have none the less tried conscientiously to support their councils' officers in the selection of sites; and some have retained the confidence of the electors in doing so. It is not possible, however, to overstate the intensity of feeling, bordering on the frenetic, aroused by a proposal to establish a site for gypsies in almost any reasonable location.

Cripps commented on two-tier government's part in the process in his paragraph 3.31:

> *Division of Functions.* The National Farmers Union and some gypsy organisations see the division of responsibilities between county and district councils as a major stumbling block in the provision of sites; and I have evidence of its becoming just this in parts of some counties. This can be due to an understandable reluctance of county councils, who are seeking to establish good relations with district councils on a basis of partnership in planning, to override their wishes . . . the district councils have no power of veto (under the planning laws), although the attitudes of some county councils give them something very close to it.

My own considered conclusion is that all local authorities should as a first priority aid and abet, through their different departments, Travellers wishing to set up their own sites, and then deal with the much more difficult problem of how one accommodates those who have been moving from place to place, sometimes all over the country. Arguing the need for generous site provision in an area of shifting and different Traveller population, does nothing to help arguments for particular site locations. If people can provide their own small sites, the arguments for larger ones will reduce considerably.

Table 2: List of designated authorities as at 31 January 1985

Type of authority	Made	Laid before Parliament	Coming into operation
London boroughs			
Barking	13/3/73	21/3/73	1/6/73
Bexley	17/4/75	25/4/75	1/7/75
Camden	27/4/81	6/5/81	27/5/81
Croydon	28/5/74	7/6/74	1/8/74
Enfield	4/3/75	13/3/75	1/6/75
Greenwich	28/5/74	7/6/74	1/8/74
Hammersmith and Fulham	1/7/75	10/7/75	1/8/75
Havering	13/3/73	21/3/73	1/6/73
Hillingdon	15/8/84	15/8/84	17/8/84
Islington	27/4/81	6/5/81	27/5/81
Kensington and Chelsea	17/4/75	25/4/75	1/6/75
Kingston-upon-Thames	10/1/84	19/1/84	10/2/84
Lambeth	3/4/79	5/4/79	26/4/79
Lewisham	3/4/79	5/4/79	26/4/79
Merton	8/5/73	16/5/73	1/8/73
Newham	13/3/73	21/3/73	1/6/73
Redbridge	13/3/73	21/3/73	1/6/73
Richmond-upon-Thames	13/12/72	21/12/72	1/4/73
Sutton	28/5/74	7/6/74	1/8/74
Waltham Forest	13/3/73	21/3/73	1/6/73
Wandsworth	5/11/81	16/11/81	7/12/81
Westminster	30/10/74	7/11/74	1/1/75
Former county boroughs			
Bolton	2/1/74	17/1/74	31/3/74
Bury	8/5/73	16/5/73	1/8/73
Leeds	8/5/73	16/5/73	1/8/73
Lincoln	2/1/74	17/1/74	31/3/74
Manchester	13/12/72	21/12/72	1/4/73
Oxford	28/5/74	7/6/74	1/8/74
Plymouth	25/9/72	4/10/72	1/1/73
St Helens	25/9/72	4/10/72	1/1/73
Stoke-on-Trent	25/9/72	4/10/72	1/1/73
Wolverhampton	13/12/72	21/12/72	1/4/73
County and district councils			
Dorset CC	17/8/78	25/8/78	21/9/78

(County and district councils, cont.)

Aylesbury Vale DC				
Chiltern DC	Bucks	16/9/81	23/9/81	14/10/81
South Bucks DC				
West Sussex CC		25/1/82	3/2/82	24/2/82
High Peak BC, Derbys		25/1/82	3/2/82	24/2/82
Kennet				
North Wiltshire	Wilts	25/1/82	3/2/82	24/2/82
Thamesdown				
W Wiltshire				
Milton Keynes, Bucks		1/9/82	13/9/82	5/10/82
Dartford, Kent		21/10/82	4/11/82	26/11/82
South Bedfordshire, Beds		1/11/82	11/11/82	3/12/82
Oswestry, Shropshire		13/12/82	22/12/82	13/1/83
Nuneaton and Bedworth, Warwickshire		11/3/83	23/3/83	14/4/83
Oldham, Greater Manchester		11/3/83	23/3/83	14/4/83
Hyndburn, Lancashire		15/3/83	24/3/83	15/4/83
Luton, Beds		5/8/83	17/8/83	8/9/83
Trafford, GMC		5/9/83	15/9/83	7/10/83
Ashford, Kent		13/9/83	22/9/83	14/10/83
Salisbury, Wilts		13/9/83	22/9/83	14/10/83
Gravesham, Kent		22/12/83	12/1/84	3/2/84
Rochdale, GMC		23/2/84	5/3/84	27/3/84
South Derbyshire		11/7/84	19/7/84	13/8/84
Boston, Lincolnshire		12/9/84	20/9/84	12/10/84
West Lindsey, Lincolnshire		14/11/84	23/11/84	15/12/84
Selby, North Yorkshire		19/11/84	29/11/84	21/12/84
Huntingdon, Cambridgeshire		14/12/84	4/1/85	26/1/85
Wealden DC				
Rother DC	East Sussex	17/12/84	4/1/85	26/1/85
Eastbourne DC				
Hastings DC				
Chester, Cheshire		14/12/84	4/1/85	26/1/85

References

Caravans Sites and Control of Development Act 1960, HMSO.

Caravan Sites Act 1968, HMSO; see also a report of the joint working party of the Local Authority Associations and the National Gypsy Council, August 1971, which is out of print but available from local authority officers if they will photocopy it.

Local Government Act 1972, Section 190, HMSO.

Local Government Planning and Land Act 1980, Sections 70, 173-6 inclusive, 187; Schedules 3, 34, HMSO.

Compulsory Purchase Orders: A Guide to Procedure, Department of the Environment, 1978.
Department of the Environment Circular 8/81, including Annex 2, HMSO.
Home Office Circular 8/81, phone (01) 213 6315 for copies.

Sites Provided by Local Authorities in England, list from Gypsy Sites Branch, Department of the Environment, address given in Chapter 1.

Report of Debate on the Designation of Camden and Islington London Boroughs, Third Standing Committee on Statutory Instruments, *Hansard,* June 1981, HMSO.

Bennett and Others v Secretary of State for Wales and West Glamorgan County Council, Queen's Bench Division, 21 July 1981, transcript from Barnett, Lenton and Co, phone (01) 405 2345.
Brown and Gilson Estates v Secretary of State for the Environment and Another, Queen's Bench Division, 13 December 1978, transcript from Walsh, Cherer and Co, phone (01) 242 7057.

Kensington and Chelsea London Borough Council v Wells and Others, Court of Appeal, 1973, *Local Government Reports* 289.
R v Secretary of State for the Environment and Cheshire County Council *ex parte* Halton District Council, (on Section 8 of the Caravan Sites Act 1968), in *The Times*, 14 July 1983.
R v Secretary of State for the Environment and the London Borough of Hammersmith and Fulham *ex parte* Ward, High Court, 1983, in *The Times*, 6 October 1983.

Commissioner for Local Administration, Wales: Complaint against Swansea, Decision 8/6/81, CN 80/69; England: London: Brent, Inv. 3960S: Hackney, Inv. 2861S; Islington, Inv. 196/S/78; Tower Hamlets, Inv. 632/S/77.
Outside London: Hampshire and Rushmoor Borough, Inv. 701/J/81; Kent, Inv. 3969S; Epsom and Surrey, Inv. 4534S, from Commission for Local Adminstration, 21 Queen Anne's Gate, London SW1H 9BU, phone (01) 222 5622.
Rejected Complaint against Avon County Council for Lack of Site Provision, Parliamentary Commissioner for Administration, 1977.

R.K. Home, 'The Caravan Sites Act 1968: Progress and Problems with Designation', *Journal of Planning and Environment Law*, April 1984, p. 226.

Streamlining the Cities; government proposals for reorganising local government in Greater London and the Metropolitan Counties, Cmnd. 9063, HMSO.
Which? Magazine, March 1978, has an excellent pictorial guide to local government, from the Consumers Association, 1 Caxton Hill, Hertford SG13 7LZ, phone Hertford 57773 or (01) 839 1222.

6. Protection of caravan and site residents

Since 1968, Travellers on private commercial sites have enjoyed the same increasing protection from eviction as other caravan site dwellers on private commercial sites. This protection began with Part I of the same Caravan Sites Act 1968 which established local authorities' duty to provide Traveller sites. The Act also established basic protection from harassment and sudden eviction for all caravan site residents, but gave residents of private commercial sites who rented pitches more protection than those on local authority sites. Courts could delay legal eviction of the former, but not the latter.

The Mobile Homes Act 1975 extended the rights of private site residents considerably, by requiring site operators to offer contracts to all their present and future site residents. The Mobile Homes Act 1983 not only extended protection so that the resident may not even be able to be evicted by a new site owner, but also extended protection to local authority site residents, too. That is apart from Traveller sites.

Who is protected

What follows details the protection that Travellers have, in different circumstances, in ascending order of protection; in general, the further you have to read for your position, the more protection you have.

Travellers on the roadside, or on land owned by a local authority, unless a legal site, have no protection from eviction in law. Without planning permission, the local authority or highway authority (which could be the Department of Transport on major roads, or a New Town Development Corporation in a place like Basildon or Stevenage) could not set up any legal arrangement for a site. Rent and rates could not be charged and, contrary to what many people seem to believe, the families are only left on the roadside verge by the grace (or inaction) of the authority controlling the land. What tends to happen, however, is that the local authority controlling the land realises that it is its own failure to provide Traveller caravan sites, if it has this, which causes the problem. It then adopts a permissive or aggressive attitude to the encampment, depending on local pressure and the behaviour of the Travellers.

Park Street, near St Albans, is an example of such an anomaly. It is a 'tolerated' arrangement between the Department of Transport, Hertfordshire County Council and the district council, but the Travellers living on Park Street would have no protection, if it were closed.

Travellers on land owned by someone else, unless a legal site, also have no protection under any of the laws relating to caravan sites. They can be evicted by the landowner, perhaps after he has had planning enforcement action threatened or used against him. He can evict, even if he has previously charged rent, though it will take him longer through the courts if he gave permission for the Travellers to pull up in the first place.

Travellers on their own land, but without planning permission for a caravan site, also have no protection. If they cannot be evicted, they can be fined for contravening the Planning Acts (if they fail to appeal against planning enforcement action; or lose an appeal for planning permission). If they still remain on the land, against the possibility of daily fines, then they risk an injunction against them requiring them to move off. If they still don't, then they could be fined or imprisoned for contempt of a court injunction, and even have their own land taken from them and sold to pay fines and/or legal costs, with the balance of the money from the sale being paid back to them.

All Travellers, either on someone else's land or their own, do face such ultimate penalties, but few would remain on the land until they were all enforced. Those on someone else's land, in particular, would be most unlikely to find him willing to put up with the risk of the same penalties himself! They would, in practice, move off or be evicted long before.

Local authority sites

The protection, such as it is, for Travellers on local authority-run Traveller sites, is all contained in Part I of the Caravan Sites Act 1968. Neither the Mobile Homes Act of 1975 nor that of 1983 makes any effective difference at all.

Protection amounts to Section 3 of the 1968 Act, entitled 'Protection of occupiers against eviction or harassment' and, sometimes, Section 2, on minimum lengths of notice to quit. Section 3 applies to all protected caravan sites, privately or publicly run, and it outlaws:

1. illegal eviction while a contract between resident and site operator (here the local authority) exists. Subsection 1(a) uses the expression 'unlawfully deprives the occupier of his occupation', which is a very polite description for forcible eviction.
2. illegal eviction after the contract between resident and site operator had ended or been brought to an end by notice. Interestingly, subsection 1(b) specifies exclusion of the occupier 'from the protected site or from any such caravan' or the removal or exclusion of any such caravan from the site. This would seem to include those who rent both caravan and pitch, but in fact they are not protected at all by the Act, although they may be under the Rent Acts. Travellers will invariably own their own caravans, or at most rent from a friend, relative or other Traveller.
3. a situation where, during or after the end of a contract, the site operator 'with intent to cause the occupier' to give up the caravan, take it off the site, or otherwise give up his rights or fail to take action against the site operator, performs 'acts calculated to interfere with the peace or comfort of the occupier or persons residing with him'.
4. persistent withdrawal or withholding of services or facilities reasonably required for the occupation of the caravan as a residence on the site.

So we can see that Section 3 gives comprehensive protection to all residents on proper caravan sites against wrongful eviction or harassment.

The other protection Travellers may have on local authority sites is that, if they have an agreement about giving notice to end their stay, Section 2 of the Act says that they shall be given four weeks clear notice, any less not being regarded as effective. In practice, their contract may not have an arrangement for notice in it, and even if it does, Section 2 does not apply to breaches of contract. So, it has been argued that if the rent is not paid, Section 2's four weeks does not apply.

Finally, it is odd that the Mobile Homes Act 1983 does not cover local authority Traveller sites. If the idea behind the Caravan Sites Act 1968 was settlement of Travellers, which may have been the case; and which also may be right or wrong in itself, why exclude Traveller sites from protections that other caravan site residents have?

The power of courts to suspend evictions for up to twelve months, introduced by the 1968 Act, has never applied to any sites operated by local authorites, Traveller sites or otherwise.

Other local authority caravan sites

Over the years, I have heard of cases of Travellers stopping on mobile home sites. Although I am sure not many Travellers do stop on these, it is worth mentioning that those who do so will get the extra benefits of the protection of the Mobile Homes Act 1983, including rights to sell the caravan on site, the right to give the mobile home to a family member, and so on, as detailed in Housing Booklet 16.

These benefits are greater than Travellers have on the sites run by local authorities.

Private sites

There are a few commercial caravan sites run by Travellers for other Travellers; a very few are run by non-Travellers. Residents on these have full rights to a contract with the operator, and the protection from eviction and harassment which applies to those on local authority sites, with the additional powers of a court to suspend eviction for up to twelve months after the residential contract has ended.

Shortage of space prevents me going into fuller detail, but briefly, exactly the same protections apply to Traveller residents on private Traveller sites as apply to residents of any other private caravan site, with no differences of the sort that exist in the public sites sector.

Protection under the Rent Acts

It is worth mentioning that protection for those who rent the caravan, as well as the pitch, from the site owner is not covered by the Mobile Homes Act, but that such residents may be protected by the Rent Acts.

Holiday caravan site residents are not protected at all by the

Mobile Homes Acts or Caravan Sites Act 1968. But where protection exists for a resident, he can usually take a site owner to a court or arbitrator to decide the issue. For wrongful eviction or harassment, the local authority can prosecute the site owner, as both are criminal offences.

References

Caravan Sites Act 1968, HMSO.
Mobile Homes Act 1975, HMSO.
Mobile Homes Act 1983, HMSO.

Mobile Homes: A Guide for Residents and Site-Owners, Housing Booklet No. 16, Department of the Environment, July 1983.

Report of the Mobile Homes Review, HMSO, 1977.

7. Why and how are Travellers moved on?

To begin with, it is worth remembering that Travellers will often move from one stopping-place to another for reasons of their own. These include: work opportunities some distance away, such as fruit picking in summer or potatoes in autumn, in rural areas; social reasons, such as wanting to be nearer a family member in need, weddings, funerals, or falling out with friend or relative; prospects of work elsewhere; the unsuitability of a stopping-place, such as too much mud on a verge, so that the lorry gets stuck, a site too dangerous for children, a sudden illness or accident that is blamed on the site, mess caused by others; or the arrival of undesirable neighbours. Families may also move because of pressure from local people, who are unfriendly, nasty or even threatening; or when another group of Travellers arrives, or threaten to arrive, and the group already there decides it is in its best interests to move. Finally, there is legal action, or the prospect of it, which may bring an encampment or site to an end. There are many different factors which affect the decisions and action which can result in Travellers being evicted, but the main ones are:

1. Where they are camped
2. Who owns the land
3. Whether the owner allows them to be there
4. How many caravans, people and animals there are
5. The activities being carried on
6. How waste is being disposed of
7. The habits of the Travellers (noise late at night? children upsetting neighbours? damage or violence definitely caused by the Travellers?)
8. The attitude of the local police
9. Whether the Travellers are known and accepted locally

The attitudes of both Travellers and their neighbours are absolutely vital to the whole process. The willingness of Travellers not to upset their neighbours and the willingness of the neighbours to seek practical solutions to problems which do occur can make all the difference. Local people should not feel that a constructive approach prejudices their future right to complain, or perpetuates the encampment or makes it likely to be a site.

Own land

A Traveller on his or her own land is in a rather different position from others. Neighbours may view a fellow-landowner and fellow-ratepayer as at first an unknown quantity. Although there may be objections by a neighbour to planning permission being granted, there is not (usually!) the same telephone call to the local council to ask for the Travellers to be 'moved instantly', or the letter to the local councillor twenty-four hours after the call to the council asking why nothing has been done (usually meaning physical eviction).

Planning permission is, as we saw earlier, the only obstacle for a landowning Traveller, but it can be a big one. If no application for planning permission is put in to the council, then neighbour complaints may well be what prompts the local planning committee to decide to serve an enforcement notice. It's important to note that, in my experience, most planning departments visit the landowning Traveller first, to explain the position. Unfortunately, they also quite often discourage an application by saying that it is unlikely to be successful. Planning officers may in addition not understand what it means to be unable to read and write, and have to depend on paying others to help you with planning applications and other paperwork.

If no application for permission is made, the planning committee does not have to decide to serve an enforcement notice, and some do not immediately do so. When it is served, however, it must be complied with or appealed against, as detailed.

Landowner allows encampment

Travellers working for a farmer can stop on his land while they are doing so. In certain other cases, short stops on pieces of land, especially large ones, are allowed under the First Schedule to the 1960 Caravan Sites Act.

In all other cases, a landowner risks two things by letting Travellers, or anyone else in a caravan, stop on his land. The first is planning enforcement action, and the second prosecution for running a caravan site without a licence. Under the first, the landowner faces the same problems as the Traveller who owns the land. He can apply for permission for a site, appeal against an enforcement notice, or evict. There is only one other alternative, but I have met several examples of it. That is where land ownership is unknown, or the owner keeps quiet. If there is no ratepaying occupier of the land, or the owner deals through agents, it is virtually impossible to trace freehold ownership against the owner's wishes, even in London and other urban areas of title registration. But the Planning Acts do allow the local planning authority to proceed against squatting Travellers, as 'occupiers'. Under the second case, any landowner can be prosecuted under Section 1 of the 1960 Act for running a site without a licence, but it is a criminal case, and the criminal standard of proof is 'beyond reasonable doubt'. The case of Bromsgrove District Council v Carthy in 1975 decided that a landowner could not necessarily be expected to pay for an eviction from his land in order to show that he did not agree with the caravans being there. Just because there are caravans on someone's land does not mean that they are guilty of running a site without a licence.

Few landowners are popular with their neighbours for setting up a Traveller caravan site on their land, and the risks of legal action are an additional deterrent. So there are few landowners who do so. If a landowner does, Travellers must regard it as merely a brief rest, which can end as soon as the owner is threatened with legal action.

Landowner does not allow encampment

Some landowners will allow Travellers they know to stop for a set period of time, say part of a year, either by special agreement, or by not taking action to move them on. Others may collect rent from families, sometimes secretly, in return for allowing them to stay. Others again may first allow Travellers to stay, but then change their minds.

If there is a long arrangement with a landowner, and Travellers have no wish to upset him regarding the future, they may well move off as soon as he asks. But if no permission has been given, is it worth sitting tight? There is no exact answer to this question which fits every case. Some private landowners, especially those who are companies and those who own a lot of land, will take some time to take any action, and will only do so when the pressure is on them from one direction or another. Others will try to force Travellers off by locking them into a field, or digging a trench round them or some other similar form of pressure. Others still will go straight to the courts and ask for a quick hearing.

Legal action by landowner

Although a landowner does not have to go to the courts, but can evict a trespasser from his land himself using 'reasonable force', it is far wiser to go to court, and get the help of the sheriff (High Court) or bailiffs (County Court) to carry out an eviction when a court order has been obtained.

In 1970, a new 'speedy procedure' was introduced to deal with cases of squatting. Order 113 of the rules of the Supreme Court and Order 26 of the County Court rules were amended to make it possible for landowners to recover their land from people whose names, or all of whose names, they did not know. Until about 1974, it was necessary for efforts to have been made to find out the names of the squatters, before the order for possession was granted. The procedure has been speeded up over the years, and the position now is that Order 24 is used by the County Court. The landowner must include in the originating application any names that he knows of those occupying the land. If they first entered it lawfully, the court can postpone the order; otherwise they cannot. The warrant for possession has to be issued within three months of the order, or the matter comes back to court. In the case of a private landowner, there is probably little point in fighting an eviction, unless a point is being made for publicity purposes. But with other landowners, the position could be different.

District or borough council as landowner

Some district councils in counties are 'borough' councils, especially in metropolitan counties, a reminder of the former county borough and metropolitan borough system which existed until 1974, as already mentioned. District councils have powers to provide caravan sites, and they also share duties over Traveller site provision with their county. If they are opposing the provision of a site in their area, it may be worthwhile fighting them if they try and evict Travellers from a piece of land that the district don't need immediately, and where the Travellers are causing no real problems.

District councils are also housing authorities, through their housing departments, or their equivalent. That means they may have duties towards people they evict, under the Housing (Homeless Persons) Act 1977.

County council as landowner

The primary duty for Traveller site provision outside London rests with county councils. Some have provided proper sites, while as observed already, Dorset and West Sussex have had their whole areas designated; other counties have part of theirs covered by designation orders. In designated areas, there is probably little point in fighting an eviction, from a publicity point of view, unless the designation was arguably wrongly given, or should be revoked. Many counties, however, have a shortage of legal sites, and in some cases an almost total lack. (The reasons for the delays have been dealt with in Chapter 5, on local authority sites.)

Essex and certain other counties, such as Surrey, have a policy of not evicting Traveller families from land that they own or control, unless there are good reasons for doing so. Essex's policy has been interpreted to mean that eviction of Travellers does not take place 'unless there are exceptional social, environmental or planning reasons for doing so'. An unacceptable road safety hazard, land being sold with vacant possession, or land needed immediately for another purpose would all be good reasons for moving families on, as would serious friction with adjacent or nearby occupiers, or waste disposal problems which could not be dealt with while Travellers remained on the encampment.

If a county council is evicting from its land while dragging its heels over site provision, and especially if there seems to be no good reason for the eviction, it may well be worth contesting the eviction, through the courts and publicity.

London authority as landowner

Each London borough has duties both under the Housing (Homeless Persons) Act 1977 and to provide Traveller sites under the Caravan Sites Act 1968. As mentioned, however, the duty to provide sites is limited to spaces for just 15 caravans, and around 20 of the 32 London boroughs are designated.

Those facing eviction by a London borough council that has not provided 'adequate accommodation' and has not been designated might feel it worthwhile to fight. Barnet, Hackney and Haringey are just three examples of boroughs which have no sites in their area as at September 1983.

Ken Livingstone, leader of the Greater London Council, has said publicly that the GLC will not evict Travellers from GLC land. Although the GLC has no duty or powers to provide any caravan sites, it is a large landowner throughout the London area.

Landowning authority's area designated

The powers granted by a designation order are additional to the ordinary powers of eviction that a landowner has. So a council that has Travellers on its land in a designated area, can either go through the magistrates court for a fine, or an order entitling it to remove them, or both, or go through the County Court (if the value of the land is low) or the High Court (if the value of the land is high, or if the authority decides to use it).

There is no special magic about a designation order. It just acts as a deterrent to those Travellers thinking of moving to the area, because it gives the local council for the area powers (if they want to pay to use them) to prosecute or evict much more quickly and easily.

If a Traveller decides to remain and fight designation powers, legal aid may be available for defending the prosecution for stopping in a designated area, if he has been prosecuted, as it is a criminal offence, and civil legal aid may be available for defence against action for the removal of the caravans.

Numbers of caravans and people

It is quite clear to me that the numbers of caravans and people on an encampment directly influences the pressure for them to be moved: I would be surprised if it didn't. But the general public is not aware of the many reasons for Travellers choosing certain stopping-places. Many people assume that if they don't protest about a Traveller encampment, then it will grow and grow. In practice, my experience is that there are two reasons for encampments to grow: one is that the land is especially suitable (hard-standings, especially during the winter months, or close to a water supply, good work prospects, shops, schools etc., or well off the road), and the other is that there are families in the area who can make use of it. It is a myth to believe that all encampments which are not ended quickly increase in size. Quite simply, there are not enough Travellers to go round them all!

Certain groups of Travellers, like the Sheridans and many of

60

the long-distance Irish Travellers, do travel in large groups, and their groupings split and re-form regularly. Several groups comprising one or two extended families each may sometimes split from a larger group and move to different places. If one of these places appears more suitable, more roomy and perhaps less easy to evict from than the others, then as many as possible may move to it. That produces a much larger number of caravans in one place. The surrounding inhabitants, who in urban areas, especially, may live close by, see a few caravans one day, then a greater number a day or two later. Without any practical problems arising, they are understandably apprehensive; elderly people living alone, single women and others who feel vulnerable at the best of times may be terrified by the unknown group who have landed at the bottom of the garden. If there is no-one who can be contacted to act as intermediary (no Gypsy Liaison Officer, local site warden, National Gypsy Council or Romany Guild representative, or experienced person from a voluntary organisation who knows that particular group of Travellers or has dealt with similar situations), and no legal site to direct the Travellers to, then they are likely to be evicted quickly, however well they behave. When that happens to them again and again, not only do they remain in large groups, but their incentive to avoid causing problems becomes non-existent. Who would struggle to stop irritation, annoyance or inconvenience to their neighbours if they knew that the neighbours were fighting against a site for them and were able to get them moved on?

Lack of control of children is the biggest practical problem with numbers in my experience. Babies and toddlers are usually kept under close surveillance, but children of school age not at school can wander off on occasion, and there is evidence that some children under ten (or who claim to be) are used for petty criminal activities that the criminal law does not allow them to be prosecuted for, and where evidence of who is using them can be hard to come by. But such instances are rare amongst Travellers as a whole, and should be kept in perspective and not quoted out of context. The bigger overall problem is lack of space to play, and use of the surrounding land. Farmers get understandably furious when their fields are littered with toys just before the combine harvester is due to go through. The farmer knows he pays the bill not just for the new combine blades, but also for the loss of use of the machine at prime harvesting time when it may be threatening to rain.

The problem which has given me most worries, however, is

children playing close to the road, or on it, even near a blind corner. There is an air of unreality about some of those situations; an apparent lack of fear by children and parents that any accident will happen – until it does, when they will probably move on quickly, effectively blaming the place for the accident.

Activities

An encampment of scrap-dealing Travellers will almost invariably get more complaints than any other, size for size, unless none of the scrap is stored or sorted on the encampment, or the place is tucked away out of public sight. And complaints are also great concerning any type of business conducted from an encampment, or where evidence of business elsewhere can be seen, such as trees which have been felled, or spoil dug out by tarmac operators, and dumped near caravans. Those who complain are quite rightly annoyed that Travellers seem to be allowed to carry on activities forbidden to anyone else. But present means of enforcement are not helpful. There is a general public demand for disposal of a mountainous number of old cars every year, and the re-use of the good parts of them. Unlike the many unemployed in the country, Travellers who make a living from scrap and the like do not depend on social security, for if they do, they risk prosecution for fraud or false claiming, and they are likely to continue to operate their business in another place.

In counties, districts may threaten to prosecute their county council for running a site without a licence. But a county council no longer needs a licence to run a Traveller site on its land. It will be interesting to see if any district council will try prosecuting a county for an encampment for which the county has not granted planning permission, and what happens to such a case.

District councils may also threaten planning enforcement against the county council, but I know of no case where this has been pursued to the full.

Local residents may also pursue a nuisance action against the owners of land. The word 'nuisance' has a special legal meaning rather stronger than the ordinary one. The law of nuisance is very complex, involving the common law of tort, statutory provisions such as parts of the Public Health Act 1936, and the possibility of civil actions in the High Court or County Court for private individual landowners affected by nuisance from their neighbour's land, as well as criminal prosecutions for public nuisances which can be brought by the Attorney-General after complaint by at least ten local people affected by it.

Two instances illustrate how nuisance cases can cause the eviction of Traveller families and their caravans. The first is a case which occurred in 1980. The county council concerned owned a piece of land which was occupied without permission by Traveller families who had been stopping in the same area for many years. The county council decided to set up a temporary site at the encampment, and began trenching to form boundaries, planning water supplies and so on. Local residents complained to the local magistrates under the Public Health Act 1936, and they found the case proved against the council as landowners who had permitted noise from generators and dogs to continue unchecked. The Magistrates Court ordered the county council first to abate the nuisance within four weeks, and secondly to prevent re-occupation of the land within eight weeks.

Although the court order did not specify eviction of the Traveller families, that had to happen in practice. The Travellers, who imagined that the temporary site idea had just been a deception by the county council, stayed on the site until physically evicted at seven o'clock one August morning.

The second instance was the High Court's decision in Page Motors v Epsom and Ewell Borough Council in Surrey. This case was on a much bigger scale. Page Motors are garage owners, and Traveller families occupied council land next to it. Page Motors claimed in a private nuisance case in court that their customers had been put off from visiting them by activities on the Traveller encampment, and that the garage had lost profits and suffered inconveniences such as smoke from tyre-burning, noise and other problems; it claimed damages. The court awarded 'substantial damages' because Epsom Council, although it had no duty to provide a Traveller caravan site, had a power to do so under the 1960 Act. Even though Page Motors would not have been able to force Epsom to set up such a site, it could still argue successfully that Epsom could have eliminated the long-running nuisance for it by using the local authority site provision powers. The case is an important and interesting one, although my fear is that it is more likely to lead to swifter evictions by local authorities under theat of nuisance proceedings, rather than to more official sites being provided.

In conclusion, it is clear that the activities of Traveller caravan-dwellers will directly influence the length of stop they are allowed on unauthorised encampments. Pressure for removal is likely to increase with size of encampment, number of vehicles and material additional to the caravans, and visibility to local residents and/or passers-by.

The law of health nuisances is well covered by the Public Health Advisory Service Practice Note 16. Virtually all the relevant law is contained in cases over private nuisance and cases interpreting the Public Health Act 1936, Control of Pollution Act 1974 (which supersedes some of the 1936 Act). The consolidating Act is the Control of Pollution 1974, which not only creates such offences as the burning of cable in the open air to extract wire from it (Section 78 of the Act), but will also finally replace some of the Public Health Act 1936, including the law of refuse collection duties and refuse disposal duties. In counties, districts have a duty to collect the various types of household, trade and commercial waste material; while counties have a duty to dispose of the waste. In Essex, for example, the Highways Department runs civic amenity sites. The 1974 Act was brought into force bit by bit, but most parts of it are now law. The Refuse Disposal (Amenity) Act 1978 deals with the law on abandoned cars and so on, and replaced the earlier Civic Amenities Act and other law on the subject, putting it all into one Act of Parliament.

In practice, the above laws tend to be important only after the Traveller caravans have left. Many Travellers dispose of their own waste properly and leave the verges where they have stopped as if they hadn't been there, apart, perhaps, from the remains of a fire, however much scrap and other bits and pieces may have been there during their stay. Some local authorities, sensibly, instead of moving on families as a result of a bit of visible scrap or actual mess, provide refuse collection. Some families are messy, and leave lots of waste behind them. But they are rarely successfully prosecuted under the law. That would require them to remain in an area until a case came up. What is really crucial is that local people want them to go, rather than stay. In my experience, pressures to move (including the threat of being prosecuted) together with physical evictions, happen much more often than prosecutions under the Litter Act or similar laws. I have met the threat of prosecution for having a fire near a highway (burning rubbish, as it happened!) but no actual case of it. After families move, the authorities argue about who clears up.

Types of land

Commons

The law of common land and the 'commonable rights' which make them so must be the most confusing area of land law in England. The only guide to the subject that I know of is *An Outline of the Law Relating to Common Land* by Morris and Ryan (Sweet and Maxwell, 1967).

Broadly, the position is that certain people traditionally used to obtain the 'fruits' of certain pieces of land. For centuries, from medieval times until the end of the nineteenth century, the common law (case law made by judges) regulated how those rights of enjoyment of grass, wood etc., on land could make it a common. Towards the end of the last century, certain Acts of Parliament set aside certain piece of land as commons, with restrictions on what the landowners could do with them.

Parliament decided in 1965 that the whole system needed reviewing and revising. The Commons Registration Act of 1965 broadly introduced the idea that the rights of common which existed and were still used should be registered. If they were not, then they would cease to be able to be used, and the landowners would have no further restrictions on their use of the land. The position is much more complicated than that, but this is a broad outline. It is important to note that it is only things which *grow* on the land, or the use of the land for certain purposes, which can be enjoyed as a 'right of common'. It does not seem to be possible to prove any rights to put a caravan on a common.

The question of whether you can 'squat' on a common in a caravan, and gain title of possession against a freehold owner by twelve years' adverse possession without ever acknowledging the superior title of the freehold owner does not seem to have been decided.

It is also not clear whether you can acquire planning rights on commons, such as established use rights. If Travellers camp on a common, they risk prosecution under Section 193 of the Law of Property Act 1925, which makes it an offence to drive on a common, or camp or light a fire. Under Section 23 of the Caravan Sites Act 1960, a local district council can, before their arrival, pass a resolution to ban caravans on all or that part of the common that Travellers have stopped on. There is also, it would seem, a possibility of eviction by the owner of the land over which the common rights exist.

Section 193 explains itself. Section 23 is a continuation of powers first given to local councils by the Commons Act 1899, Part I, under which many schemes were set up for the management and regulation of commons, and by-laws were authorised. If the local council has passed a resolution to ban caravans on all or part of a common, those who park there face a maximum £20 fine in the Magistrates Court. In turn, the council has a duty to publicise its resolution on the common itself, so that people are warned of the offence. A pity that little account was taken of those who cannot read! Finally, with all these powers in existence, it may be small wonder that I never heard of a landowner evicting from a common until August 1983 when a district council which had also brought the land tried to so in Inskip, Lancashire. The case is due to be decided in Autumn 1984, with the Travellers currently using the land intermittently, to avoid falling foul of the present order banning their use.

Highways

'Once a highway, always a highway' and 'dedication' are two expressions which can be confusing. The first is not necessarily true nowadays. Land may be 'dedicated' for use as a public highway while needed, and then 'de-dedicated' when a new road replaces it. The resulting lay-by, dead-end, or spare piece of old road is often used by Travellers, who welcome the hard-standing and easy access to a main road. But then, after a public procedure has been gone through, the highway may be closed, broken up, or transferred to other use by the highway authority (county council, GLC or London borough, or Department of Environment for major trunk roads like the A1) or another department of the same local council or government. The land must be offered back to the previous owner in most cases of recent discontinued roads, when the authority which brought it no longer needs it.

Contrary to much popular belief, the 'highway' usually includes not just the hard-surfaced carriageway but also the verge on either side, and pavement, if any. The law is now gathered together in the Highways Act 1980, plus an important minor change for Travellers, Section 187 of the Local Government, Planning and Land Act 1980. That change removed the word 'gypsy' from Section 150 of the Highways Act 1980. Section 150 was previously Section 127 of the Highways Act 1959. Under it, countless Travellers were prosecuted for 'encamping on the highway'. Many more had been prosecuted as far back as 1835 when the offence was first invented. Now it is not possible for the police and courts to prosecute just for 'being a gypsy . . . encamping on the highway', although in some areas it is still threatened.

Other sections of the Highways Act 1980 are, however, usable. Travellers are prosecuted for obstruction of the highway, for example, or for erecting structures on it. The highway authority also has power, through the civil courts (County Court or High Court) to recover possession of a highway it manages and controls.

There is no doubt that letting Travellers stop on highway verges conflicts with the duty of the council which is the highway authority, to keep highways clear. But an enlightened county such as Essex takes the view that caravans should not be automatically moved, but only where the situation warrants it. The price of the endless moving on of Traveller families, whoever does it, is more mess and less-co-operation.

Injunctions

I have met a few cases of local authorities applying for injunctions against named Travellers. The idea of an injunction is usually to stop particular people stopping on any part of your land. Salford used them in 1973, when they had evaded their duty to provide a site. I have met two other instances in Essex, in 1980 and 1982, and I know of several other instances in other parts of the country, such as in West Yorkshire.

To Travellers, the benefit of being named in an injunction is that it proves you were in the area, but few Travellers hold on to the relevant court papers. The disadvantage is that an injunction may prohibit a return to a good stopping-place, or even to several pieces of land.

If a landowner is arguing for an injunction covering more than one piece of his land, it is worth going to court and arguing firstly, that the injunction should not be spread so wide and/or, that it is unnecessary.

Local acts

Numerous Local Acts of Parliament, some of them from last century, regulate matters including the parking of caravans, in the areas they cover. They usually go through Parliament as Private Bills, and there is often no publicity. They are difficult to find out about, so it's best to ask the local council first, then try specialist solicitors in London who act as Parliamentary Agents, such as Sharpe, Pritchard and Co. These Bills are difficult to challenge when passing through Parliament.

Local legislation is, however, currently being reviewed. Under Section 262(9) of the Local Government Act 1972, the metropolitan counties are meant to have produced 'rationalisation' Acts allowing them to keep those local laws still thought to be important. This process was meant to have been completed by the end of 1979, but they were allowed extra time. The shire (non-metropolitan) counties originally had until the end of 1984, but this has now been extended to 1 April 1986. London is not involved at all.

It is worth finding out if a particular county council wants to hold on to sections of old Acts used against Travellers. Small groups can win – a branch of the Ramblers' Association in South-West England, and a Transport 2000 Group in Reading are just two organisations who challenged, and got changed, a draft Private Bill on local matters. And the National Council for Civil Liberties has considerable expertise on the subject, as a result of lobbying over clauses designed to restrict local rights to demonstrate.

An example of local legislation which could be (or is) used against Travellers is Section 36 of the Salford Corporation Act 1973, under which a maximum fine of £20 can be imposed for causing or permitting a mechanically propelled vehicle on land after the corporation has put up a sign prohibiting it. If the landownder agrees, the land can include:

> any land which appears to the Corporation to be intended for redevelopment and to be for the time being derelict and the subject or likely to be the subject of unauthorised use by the public for the parking of vehicles.

That sounds like half of Salford. Let us hope Section 36 is not re-enacted by Greater Manchester.

Section 35 of the Orpington District Council Act 1954 enables the council to apply to the Magistrates Court for an order prohibiting moveable dwellings in an area

> where it appears to the Council . . . that the amenities of any part of the district are prejudicially affected by the presence of or conditions arising from any moveable dwelling or moveable dwellings in the district.

In spite of the wording, a prosecution under the Act has been successfully defended.

By-laws

It is very difficult to find out which of the multitude of by-laws currently in force apply to the parking of caravans. By-laws have to be made under an Act of Parliament which gives the power to make them. British Rail has such a power, as do various other bodies, but most will be under the control of local authorities. The best way of finding out about them tends, unfortunately, to be by being prosecuted under one.

There is one 'model' by-law (that is, government-approved, through the Department of the Environment and/or the Home Office) which is used by many counties and boroughs, and referred to in paragraph 2.8 of the Cripps Report. It says:

> No gypsy or squatter or other such person dwelling in a tent, boat, shed or similar structure or in a van, caravan, or similar vehicle, shall occupy any land within 300 yards of any dwelling house so as to cause injury, disturbance or annoyance to the inmates of such house after being requested to depart by any inmate of the house or by his servant or by any constable on his behalf.

Perhaps the time is now ripe for reconsidering this antiquarian by-law. Who is the 'other such person' after 'gypsy or squatter'? What happens if he or she owns the next door land? Who can afford servants to tell Travellers to move off, these days? The government should think again on how 'model' this by-law is in 1984.

Flowery footnote

There is no doubt that, in some places, special efforts will be made to keep the area free of Traveller caravans. It may be through action by police, local authority officers or others. It may stem from the actions of someone with influence. Travellers usually know where they are going to encounter bother, from bitter personal experience!

The most trivial reason for asking families to move that I have met is that the verge should not be compressed by their vehicles and caravans . . . because it would prevent orchids growing there in the spring. When spring in fact came, the orchids didn't, and the Travellers who had moved complained!

References

Animals Act 1971 (on liability of owners and finders), HMSO.
Caravan Sites and Control of Development Act 1960, Sections 1 and 23, HMSO.
Control of Pollution Act 1974, HMSO (not yet all in force).
Commons Registration Act 1965, HMSO.
Highways Act 1980, HMSO.
Law of Property Act 1925, Section 193, HMSO.
Refuse Disposal (Amenity) Act 1978, HMSO.
Scrap Metal Dealers Act 1964, HMSO.
Town and County Planning Act 1971, HMSO.

Department of the Environment Circular 23/83.
80 *Local Government Reports* 727, on Section 143, 1980; see also *Journal of Planning and Environment Law* 1983, p. 108.

Bromsgrove District Council v Carthy, Divisional Court, 1975 (30), *Planning and Compensation Reports* 34.
Manchester Corporation v Connolly and Others, 1970 (1), *All England Law Reports* 961.
McPhail v Persons Unknown, 1975 (3), *All England Law Reports* 393.
Page Motors v Epsom Borough Council, 1982 (80), *Local Government Reports* 337.
R v Welwyn and Hatfield Council *ex parte* Brinkley, 1982, Commission for Local Administration in England, Complaint against Durham City Council, 426/C/79, Commission address in Chapter 5.
Scarborough Borough Council v Adams and Others, *Times Law Report*, 4/7/83.

Order 24, *County Court Rules, White Book of County Court Practice*, updated periodically.
Order 113, *Rules of the Supreme Court*, updated periodically.

County Councils Gazette, August 1983, p. 149, from Association of County Councils, Eaton House, 66A Eaton Square, London SW1 9BH, phone (01) 235 1200.

Disposal of Abandoned Vehicles, Shaw and Sons, 1981.

P. Clayden, *Our Common Land: the Law and History of Commons and Village Greens,* from the Open Spaces Society, 25a Bell Street, Henley-on-Thames, Oxfordshire RG9 2BA.

National Council for Civil Liberties, 21 Tabard Street, London SE1, phone (01) 403 3888.

Public Health Advisory Service Practice Note 16, 1978. (PHAS no longer in existence; copies from Jim Parish, The White House, Searby, Lincolnshire DN38 6BH; enclose £2 for photocopying and postage.)

8. Education

This chapter deals with the law, mechanics and financing of education for Travellers. It is very useful to have to hand a copy of the HMI discussion paper *The Education of Travellers' Children*, (Department of Education and Science, 1983). It deals mainly with good and bad practice in Traveller education by local education authorities, but it touches too on the law, administration and finance of Traveller education.

The number of Traveller children in private school is probably tiny, so we are dealing in the main with the state system. Let us begin by defining an education authority, since it is its job to provide schools and make sure children attend them.

In Inner London boroughs, the whole area is covered by the Inner London Education Authority (ILEA), a special committee of the Greater London Council. Present government plans to get rid of the GLC would also provide powers to abolish the ILEA.

In outer London boroughs, each borough council runs education.

In metropolitan counties such as Tyne and Wear, Merseyside, Greater Manchester, South Yorkshire, West Yorkshire and the West Midlands, each metropolitan borough council is the education authority.

In shire counties, the county council is the education authority.

Each of these local education authorities (LEAs) has a duty under Section 8 of the Education Act 1944:

> to secure that there shall be available for their area sufficient schools
> (a) for providing primary education . . .; and
> (b) . . . secondary education . . .
> and the schools available for an area shall not be deemed to be sufficient unless they are sufficient in number, character and equipment to afford for all pupils opportunities for education offering such variety of instruction and training as may be desirable

in view of their different ages, abilities and aptitudes, and of the different periods for which they may be expected to remain at school including practical instruction and training appropriate to their respective need.

This is obviously a very extensive duty. How can Travellers not settled in an area benefit from it? Unfortunately, the duty of an LEA to children not 'belonging to its area' was not made clear cut until the Education Act 1980. Following the London Borough of Croydon's refusal to admit a Traveller girl to school because she was not on their official site in 1977, the Department of Education and Science wrote:

> In determining whether a family has established residence in its area for the local education authority to have an obligation to make educational provision for the children, an authority may take account of the likely duration of their stay in the area, which could be influenced by the legality of the parents' residence.

The position seems to have been defined by Section 6 of the Education Act 1980, which obliges LEAs to make arrangements enabling parents of children in their area to express a 'preference' as to the school they wish those children to attend. The HMI discussion paper mentioned above confirms that the duty applies to all parents of all children in that LEA area regardless of where they are living. If the LEA shows that admitting the child to the 'preferred' school would 'prejudice the provision of efficient education' or 'the efficient use of resources', as set out in Section 6(3), then the LEA could still have a duty to provide education for those children elsewhere, if the parents were to appeal successfully under Section 7 of the 1980 Act.

The subject is covered in more detail, in the Department of Education and Science Circular 1/81 (HMSO) and in the 1982 edition of *Traveller Education* (National Gypsy Education Council). The 1980 Act took effect at the beginning of the autumn term 1982, and later I will give a guide to using it.

Money

At the centre of any discussion about who provides what is the question of who pays. Special financing arrangements exist for Traveller children being educated inside or outside ordinary schools. The most important part of these special financial arrangements is the 'No Area Pool'. This is exactly what it says: a pool of money to pay for the education of children for whom 'no area' (that is, no LEA) is responsible. Every LEA in the country has to pay into this pool for the costs of educating 'no area' children. This is done by adjusting rate support grant from central government to each local authority. But what the 'No Area Pool' really means is that those LEAs which provide education for Traveller children use it, and those who don't provide education will still be paying towards the costs of those who do.

Originally, the pool was organised under the Education (Miscellaneous Provisions) Acts, 1948 and 1953, but it is now regulated by Section 32 of the Education Act 1980. The Education (areas to which pupils belong) Regulations 1980 (Statutory Instrument 1980, 917) and the Block Grant (Educational Adjustments) (England) Regulations 1981 (SI 1981 No. 312) give the details.

The existence of the pool means that headteachers who admit Traveller children to their schools can remind the LEA which employs them that it can claim from the pool:

1. the cost of educating in ordinary classes those Traveller children, at the full primary or secondary (depending on the type of school) Inter-Authority Payments Committee rate. The total amount depends on how many weeks each pupil has attended the school.
2. special provision for these children while they are in school. This could be extra remedial teaching help, perhaps from a peripatetic teacher of Traveller children. Everything can be charged to the pool at 75 per cent of the recurrent costs (and loan charges) actually spent while it is being used for the Traveller children, or at the current IAPC rate (see above), if that should be greater.
3. other costs actually spent on Traveller children's education (such as boarding fees) can be charged in full to the pool.

It is important to remember that these are not alternatives, and that money can be claimed for the same children being educated in ordinary classes and having special help, for example.

The above arrangements do not mean that a particular school gets the money. The school may negotiate with the LEA, often through an area education office to get extra teachers, for example.

If there is a special education system for Traveller children in an area – for example, a mobile school, a special classroom on an official site; peripatetic teachers who travel from school to school, site to site or roadside to roadside – then their cost to the LEA who employs or funds them, and any extra costs of (say) a school bus, is charged at 75 per cent of actual recurrent costs, as under (2) above.

There are increasing numbers of LEAs running schemes for Traveller children, and encouraging them into schools, but there is still a long way to go.

What parents have to do

Section 36 of the Education Act 1944, as amended by Section 17, Education Act 1981, requires the parent of every child of compulsory school age (at present, 5-16 years) to:

> cause (the child) to receive efficient full-time education suitable
> to (the child's) age, ability and aptitude, either by regular attend-
> ance at school or otherwise.

Note that this section does not absolutely force the parent to send the child to school. But it does require 'efficient full-time education' to be provided. Until a Traveller wins a court case which decides that 'education' for a Traveller child can include learning his father's trade as a major part of it, it is unlikely that any non-literate Traveller parent is going to be able to provide alternative education which satisfies an LEA.

If parents do not send their child to school, or begin to and then the child plays truant, in theory the same law applies to them as anyone else. Proceedings may be brought in the Juvenile Court; this has the power to make a 'care order' if it is satisfied that the child is in need of care and control. Or perhaps the LEA will ask for a school attendance order, requiring that the child goes to a specified school, and that the matter comes back to court if attendance is not maintained. Section 10 of the Children and Young Persons Act 1933, which is aimed at 'persons habitually wandering from place to place' who prevent children receiving 'efficient full-time education', also applies.

In practice, in my experience, sensible LEAs do not pursue any of these legal means as anything other than a last resort, and those that try them against any but the most settled and secure Travellers, living in houses or on official sites, will often find that families will move on as soon as the papers for the court case arrive, or even earlier.

I entirely agree with the firm and principled position of the National Gypsy Council, which says that Travellers should be in a position no different from anyone else's; they should have their children in the local school, and should be prosecuted if they don't. Legal proceedings should always be regarded as a means to the end of getting a child educated, not as administrative convenience, a response to pressure from local people, or revenge.

If a Traveller parent does get prosecuted for failure to send a child to school, or under Section 10 of the 1933 Act, then they may defend themselves with Section 56 of the Education Act 1944, which effectively says that children of parents whose work requires them to travel from place to place shall not have to ensure full-time attendance. As long as the child attends as often as possible, and the parent can prove at least two hundred half-day attendances, equalling a hundred days of full schooling, during the twelve months before the prosecution was begun, then the parent has a good defence. In practice, I have never met this defence being used by a Traveller, but it is there, if needed. Much more important is how children get admitted to school:

Using the Education Act 1980

School: They can't come here: they don't belong to the area.

Parent: Yes they can. The area they belong to has no connection with your duty to consider their preference for any school, under the 1980 Act, Section 6(5). What's more, if they don't belong to your area, you can reclaim the whole cost of their education from the pool. Under Section 31.

School: But we cannot afford to make any special provision for their needs.

Parent: Once again, you can reclaim the whole cost from the pool.

School: But we don't believe they will be here long enough to achieve anything useful.

Parent: That doesn't remove your duty to provide me with an opportunity to make my preference for your school known, and the duty for your authority to agree with it, if possible under Section 6(1).

School: This school is full up. Why don't you go to the area education office? I'll ring them up and let them know you're coming.

Area office   Our schools are all full up, I'm afraid.
employee:

Parent: What? All of them? But under Section 6 of the 1980 Act, Travellers have an equal right with all other parents to have their school preferences considered. You can't discriminate against me by putting me last on the list.

Area office   But our councillors do not want us to give you any support while you are camped in that lay-by. You are illegally parked!
employee:

Parent: That's not a good enough excuse. Paragraph 5 of Circular 1/81 from the Department of Education and Science says that your duty on preferences applies to all children (including mine) whether they are in the area temporarily or permanently and whether or not we are Travellers.

Area office   I'm afraid we already have a number of Traveller children in that particular school.
employee:

Parent: That's no reason, in itself, for not admitting my children. The Race Relations Act 1976 applies to your LEA just as much as it applies to others. I would suggest you look at the Brymbo case decision by the Commission for Racial Equality. (See Chapter 13)

Area office   Aren't you being evicted next week, though? Your children would just have to leave again.
employee:

Parent: No they wouldn't. We intend to stay in the area, even though we have been moved around again and again. As long as my children can get to the school they can stay on the register, under the 1956 Registration Regulations, Section 4. If you try to remove them from the register, we will appeal to the Minister of Education.

Area office   But your children haven't been in school before. With all the cuts and savings we have to make, we can't provide the extra facilities they'll need. So they'll just be wasting time at the back of the class.
employee:

Parent: In that case, I appeal for an assessment under Section 9 of the Education Act 1981. Could you arrange that, please?

Area office   That could mean we decide that one or more of them
employee: should go to a special school, you know.
Parent: They can't be treated as slow learners just because they
haven't been to school before. If we disagree with the
assessment I've just asked you for, then we'll appeal
against it under Section 8 of the 1981 Act.
Area office   Look, we are busy here. The local school is full up, but
employee: get in touch in a few days and I'll see what else can be
offered by then.
Parent: I want my children in school right away. I want them in
the local school so they can get special help with reading
and writing and catch up with the others. If you won't
organise it now, I'm appealing under Section 7 of the
Education Act 1980. I'm going to sit here until you help
me fill in the forms to do that.
Area office   That would be a lot more work for us. Hold on while I
employee: talk to the Education Officer about finding your children
a place.

The above dialogue may be slightly unlikely, but is does cover many of the arguments that may arise in practice. It also emphasises the importance of persisting in getting schooling. An increasing number of, initially, Traveller mothers, and now, increasingly, fathers are pressing for proper education for their children.

Special education

The law of special education for those with learning problems of one sort or another was overhauled by the Education Act 1981. It was referred to briefly in the dialogue above, but the best guide to the 1981 Act, which only came into force in Autumn 1982, is the *Special Education Handbook* (Advisory Centre for Education, 18 Victoria Park Square, London E2 9NP, £2 plus postage). What is clear is that the new procedures under the Act are designed:

1. to reduce the need for separate special schools
2. to enable ordinary schools to assess children with minor learning problems, and deal with them
3. to give parents full rights of challenge of assessments of their children's 'special needs' along the way.

The only disadvantage would seem to be the complexity of the procedures!

Transport

Difficulties often arise over school transport arrangements for Traveller children. To begin with, the stopping-places used by those with no site may well be tucked away from the communities which surround the local school, but not be so far away that the ILEA *has* automatically to provide transport. An LEA has to provide transport when a pupil lives more than a certain number of miles from the appropriate school, the number varying with the type of school, as follows: primary, 1½; junior, 2; secondary, 3. There is a general power to provide transport under Section 55 of the Education Act 1944, and some enlightened authorities may use this to provide transport to get Traveller children school in the first place, even though their usual policy is not to provide any unless there is the legal duty mentioned above.

What is most important is that each LEA has a clear, if not publicised, policy on transport for Traveller children to a school they may otherwise not get to, and that the policy is clearly understood by all their various central and area officers, as well as head-teachers in schools which have admitted Travellers' children who may be affected by that policy.

Discrimination

Although the possibility of discrimination by schools or the LEA has been mentioned, often produced in the form of arguments which evade the point, under pressure from (say) other parents, much more common is discrimination against children in school. This may take the form of name-calling ('gyppo', 'dirty gyppo' and the like), but I have met instances much worse, involving physical bullying and intimidation. It is important that teachers and head-teachers are keenly aware of the possibility of this arising, and of Traveller children keeping quiet about it through fear. It is a most difficult problem to overcome, but a crucial one.

References

Education Act 1944, HMSO.
Education Act 1980, HMSO.
Education Act 1981, HMSO.

Department of Education and Science Circular 1/80, especially paras 31-41.
The Education of Gypsy, Fairground and Circus Children and Others leading Nomadic Lives, series of reports on short courses run by the Department of

Education and Science, obtainable from the DES Library, Elizabeth House, York Road, London SE1 7PH.

The Education of Travellers' Children, HMI Discussion Paper, Department of Education and Science, 1983, from Room 2/11, address above.

General Traveller education matters: A, B and S11 Branches, Department of Education and Science, phone (01) 928 9222 x 2343, or visit Room 4/83.

Report on a survey of the West Midland Education Service for Travelling Children SS80/6/04 191/83 DS3/83, HM Inspectors, February and March, 1983, from DES Publications Despatch Centre, Honeypot Lane, Stanmore, Middlesex HA7 1AZ.

Peter Newell, *Special Education Handbook*, Advisory Centre for Education, 1983, 18 Victoria Park Square, London E2 8NP, phone (01) 980 4596 (The Centre also publishes other useful and readable material on education.)

Chris Reiss, *Education of Travelling Children*, Macmillan, 1976.

Dick Worrall, *Gypsy Education*, Walsall Council for Community Relations, 1979, from 60 Rowley St, Walsall WS1 2AY.

Education Report 1980, National Gypsy Council, from Greengate St, Oldham, Greater Manchester, phone (061) 665 1924.

Traveller Education (annually) National Gypsy Education Council, from Thomas Acton, phone (01) 555 3648.

Advisory Committee for the Education of Romany and other Travellers, c/o Mary Waterson, Keepers, High Wych, Sowbridgeworth, Hertfordshire, phone (0279) 722704.

A miscellany of educational materials and other publications can be obtained from: Dennis Binns, 18 South Drive, Chorltonville, Manchester 21, phone (061) 881 2411.

A recent publication of great importance is *Education for All,* Lord Swann FRSE, chairman, Cmmd. 9453, HMSO. Copies of Traveller chapter available from Mary Waterson, at the above address.

9. Housing

A statement, in paragraph 1.4 of the Cripps Report, should be the starting point of any discussion about Travellers and housing:

> Whatever the previous policies, the Secretaries of State now accept the gypsy's right to a nomadic existence for as long as he wishes to continue it. There is no intention to put pressure on him to settle or assimilate unless and until he wishes to do so; but the opportunity is to be provided.

Housing committee members in every local authority should note particularly the expression 'the opportunity is to be provided'.

There are a lot of myths about Traveller attitudes to housing. One is that a Traveller who moves into a house becomes less a Traveller, or ceases to be one altogether. This is as wrong as saying that a West Indian ceases to be West Indian by moving to Britain. Whatever may happen through lapse of time, interm. rriage and changes down the generations, the Traveller identity is far too strong and deeply-entrenched to be abandoned by a mere change of abode.

Another myth is that Travellers will all wish to have the same living arrangements, and all have the same views about how and where they live. But I know Romany families living in houses and in caravans, poor Travellers who move in and out of council housing, and Travellers who set up their own private sites and then want to build a bungalow on them. Individual choice leads to a far happier state of affairs for the Traveller, as for the rest of us, than doctrinaire philosophies about either 'assimilation' into the community by pressurising families into houses, or by refusing all applications for council housing and planning applications for private caravan sites or bungalows. I have regularly heard local authority planning officers relying on a family's council housing application, or their long-term desire to build a bungalow on their proposed caravan site, as a reason for arguing against the granting of planning permission for a particular private caravan site. It has never seemed surprising to me that, without local authority sites, Travellers apply for housing, rather than living on the roadside under continual threat of being moved on, and with newspaper publicity and/or local hostility.

This chapter looks first at ordinary council housing applications by Travellers. Then I will consider the Housing (Homeless Persons) Act 1977.

Council housing

In my experience, the policy and allocation arrangements of local authority housing departments are far more important in practice to Traveller families than the Housing (Homeless Persons) Act 1977. It is also quite clear that local housing authorities vary considerably, both in their rules for admission to housing waiting lists and their attitude to Travellers. But the rules are, as one would expect, based on the assumption that each housing authority has a first duty to house those who have been in its area longest, and least duty to house those whose caravan has just parked on the verge down the road. This is of course unless the caravan is just about to collapse and someone has to house the family under the 1977 Act.

I have found two articles particularly useful in trying to understand how the general system works, and how it works for Travellers. One is 'Gypsies and Housing Policy' by Pam Gallagher (available from me); the other is 'Allocating Housing in the 1980s' by David Hoath, (*Local Government Chronicle*, August 1980).

London Boroughs are not allowed to have 'pre-registration qualifications' for those applying for their housing lists, but the Housing Act 1980, instead of extending this ban to all housing authorities, merely required all of them to produce a free summary of their rules for admission to the list, and a full version of the rules at a reasonable cost. Faced with a Traveller family who wishes to apply for council housing, any adviser should start by finding out the rules for the housing authority areas where the family has spent most time.

It is baffling to many people, including many Travellers, that different housing authorities have different rules. I know families who will travel from one district to another because of a rumour that housing will be easier to get in another place. In a 1983 survey of Essex authorities, some had a most enlightened approach to providing sometimes short-term housing for Travellers, while others had rules which would exclude all but the most tenacious family. If one lives in a caravan, has nowhere legal to park it, and no friends or relatives to move in with, how does one stay in an area for the necessary three years, say, to qualify to go on a housing list? If counties won't agree to caravan sites for Travellers, because of district opposition, isn't it about time that county and districts discussed how to deal in the meantime with housing applications from Travellers?

Once on the housing list, a Traveller family living in an over-crowded caravan on the roadside, with no mains services, may rise quickly to its top. Then it is a question of advisers or friends keeping an eye on the housing committee to see if they allocate to the family the next appropriate vacant council house, of the size agreed for the family.

There is no doubt that council house sales, and the tiny number of new council houses built, due to central government's spending cuts and its belief in private building firms, have both contributed to a lengthening of queues in many areas and made it less and less likely that Traveller families, along with others, will soon have any relief from, say, their roadside moving-on and single-room family sleeping arrangements. In addition, even when Travellers do rise to the top of the housing list, we have seen, and will see, how discrimination conducted behind closed doors can lengthen their wait still further. What many Travellers would really like is a bungalow with space for the caravan next to it, usually just a pipe-dream.

The Housing (Homeless Persons) Act 1977

It is not possible, in this small Handbook, to go into great detail on the 1977 Act, which is in any case of limited day-to-day importance to Travellers, and then only for those wishing to use it to transfer to housing. The 1977 Act is a remarkably clear step-by-step guide to who gets which council to provide accommodation for them, and how. It was considerably altered in Parliament, with amendments from the then Opposition housing spokesman Hugh Rossi MP removing many proposed duties towards the single homeless. However, Stephen Ross, the Liberal MP who piloted it through to the statute book, can claim much credit for it.

In contrast with the tiny handful of cases under the Caravan Sites Act 1968, most of them concerning Minister's powers to force site provision, or disputes between local authorities, the Homeless

Persons Act has generated seventy cases in four years. So the law on the subject is constantly being modified by the courts, and may also be changed by Parliament in the future.

For a full examination of the Act, I would recommend the 1983 Legal Action Group paperback *The Homeless Persons Act* by Andrew Arden. At the very least, it's useful to have a copy of the Act itself and its *Code of Guidance* (1983).

Armed with these, and remembering also the expertise that the homeless people's group Shelter, has, for example, developed on the Act's working, we need to examine the importance of the Act to Gypsies.

The 1977 Act created 'The Homeless Persons' Obstacle Race', as an article in the *Journal of Social Welfare Law* called it. In order to get housing provided by a local housing authority, or help with finding it, you have to go through a number of hoops.

Hoop 1 is proving that you are 'homeless'. Travellers do so by quoting Section 1(2)(c) of the 1977 Act, by showing that they have their caravan as accommodation but that:

> it consists of a movable structure, vehicle or vessel designed or adapted for human habitation and there is no place where [the Traveller] is entitled or permitted both to place it and to reside in it.

There has never been any argument about the wording of this subsection, which reflects the small number of Traveller families which seek housing under the Act. The view of the Department of the Environment's Gypsy Sites Division (as it was then) in 1978 was that a Traveller family only became 'homeless' under the 1977 Act when it was actually evicted, because until then, simply by not being evicted, they had been 'permitted' a stay. It is arguable that a landowner can recover land by force, and that the first approach by, or on behalf of, the landowner telling a family to leave ends the 'permission' and that court proceedings due to come up on a named date mean that the family is 'threatened with homelessness', which brings the Act into force, and may put the duty of preventing 'homelessness' onto the local council. In any event, only proof that the family had somewhere else legal to put their caravan would stop it being homeless. If the family has its own private site, or reserved pitch on a local authority site, then it isn't homeless under the 1977 Act.

Hoop 2, which can only be tried for if you've passed through

Hoop 1, and proved you are homeless, is proving a 'priority need for accommodation'. Section 2 of the Act lists the four cases which mean qualification. Travellers are most likely to have a 'priority need' through having either dependent children or a pregnant woman, although it is possible that an elderly single person, or someone who is single and handicapped or disabled would be living on their own, perhaps looked after by a childless family, and that they also would qualify if 'vulnerable'. Whichever housing authority is found to have a duty to provide accommodation for the individual with the 'priority need for accommodation', if any authority is, must also provide for those who are 'residing with or might reasonably be expected to reside with' that individual.

'Priority need for accommodation' also arises where the homelessness (or threat of it) is due to an emergency (flood, fire or other disaster). I have dealt with one case of a family rehoused from a leaking tent, which the housing department dealt with immediately.

Hoop 3 is an obstacle that the housing authority have to prove against the Traveller, rather than the other way round. It is that the housing authority does not have to provide for someone who became 'homeless intentionally'. This is very important in practice, and covered by Section 17 of the Act:

> . . . a person becomes homeless intentionally if he deliberately does or fails to do anything in consequence of which he ceases to occupy accommodation which is available for his occupation and which it would have been reasonable for him to occupy.

A recent, and important, Court of Appeal case, R v Salford City Council, *ex parte* Devonport, decided that the acts or omissions which lead to someone becoming homeless did not have to be 'deliberate' in the sense of trying to cause homelessness; the person need only have intended to perform the physical acts or omissions, without being aware of the consequence.

The clear message for Travellers wanting housing which comes from both the Salford case and another, in the High Court in March 1983, involving Hammersmith and Fulham and Duro Rama, is that *all* details of movements, and reasons for them, should be given to the housing authority, if and when there is to be a reliance on the 1977 Act. If movement off an official site, for example, is apparently voluntary and unexplained, then any housing authority which finds out about it may refuse housing. Then the Travellers would have to rely on a long court battle, which they could have prevented.

The final Hoop, the fourth, decides which kind of housing an authority should provide. A 'homeless' Traveller family, with a member who has a 'priority need for accommodation', and whom the housing department is not arguing is 'intentionally homeless', has to have a 'local connection' with the area of the liable housing authority. It is something else that the housing department has to prove against the Traveller, rather than the other way round. But only one member of the family need have this 'local connection', and it is well worthwhile for the family to mention this connection when they apply. If the housing department, under Section 5, are 'of the opinion' that no such 'local connection' exists, but that someone in the family has a 'local connection' with another area, then the authority to which the family has applied can transfer the responsibility to the other one, unless the move would cause a 'risk of domestic violence' to any of those involved.

Section 18 of the Act says that a 'local connection' is a connection with an area because a person:

1. is or in the past was normally resident in it and his residence in it is or was of his own choice; or
2. is employed in it [presumably includes self-employed]
3. has family associations with it; or
4. is there 'because of any special circumstances'.

If there is to be a transfer between authorities, the Traveller or his adviser should ask for a copy of the 'notification' which the 'sending' authority must send to the 'receiving' one.

The seventy legal cases under the Act have all been for 'administrative review'. The Act itself does not spell out any procedures for challenging the actions of a local authority or any mode of appeal. Challenges have to be made using the general common law principles of review of administrative action.

These cases have thrown up many interesting points, the most important being that local authority housing policies are not necessarily legal: a policy of not housing Travellers could be challenged in the courts, for example. The *Code of Guidance* produced by the government to help local authorities and the public understand the Act is also not legally binding; the Act is always the point to come back to.

No major test cases have involved Traveller families, but the

Court of Appeal decision in R v Wyre Borough Council *ex parte* Carr ruled that the housing authority's initial decision was that the five-child family involved was not homeless while living in a motor caravan parked on a seaside promenade because the 'shelter/accommodation [was] in keeping with [the family's] chosen mode of living'. Wyre Borough Council finally secured accommodation for the family with Birmingham City Council. The Court of Appeal decided that Wyre were wrong in their initial assessment and wrong to try and move the applicant to Birmingham.

Type of accommodation

There is, unfortunately, no way of getting caravan sites provided under the Homeless Persons Act. In fact, it is more likely to produce fiercer arguments between the counties with responsibility for sites and the districts who have to provide housing. The old *Code of Guidance* said, in its Annex at Paragraph A.2.10:

> Where people are homeless because they have a caravan or houseboat but no site or mooring for it, the housing authority are not obliged to make equivalent accommodation available; in particular, there is no obligation on the district council to provide gypsy caravan sites. Where the duty to secure accommodation arises in the case of a gypsy family, the authority may arrange with the county council for a site to be made available; or they may secure some form of housing accommodation.

The 1977 Act seems to have been most used as a defence against eviction by landowner authorities which have a duty under it. It is still well worth challenging an arbitrary Traveller eviction by a London borough or district council, by reminding them of their duties under the Act to any of the families due for eviction, for they would go cleanly through all the Act's hoops.

No-one knows how many Travellers live in houses, council or private. 'Most guesses say that there is a Traveller in a house for every one in a caravan or tent', wrote Jeremy Sandford in his 1973 book *Gypsies* (Abacus). A few reports quoted by Pam Gallagher in her article give evidence of Irish Travellers settling in Sparkbrook, Birmingham and Manchester, but information is patchy.

Perhaps the final word on this subject should be left to Jimmy Penfold, quoted by Jeremy Sandford in *Gypsies:*

We moved into a house because things were so bad on the road . . .
when I'm in bed, I have to be underneath the window, I can't
sleep in a closed room. I've got to look out at the sky. I'm a Gypsy
. . . you can't put a wild bird in a cage and expect it to live . . . I was
talking to quite a few [Gypsies] and there's a hell of a lot of them
coming out of the houses . . . living in a house you can't get what
you want and how you want it . . . The world could be a garden of
Eden if men would only live and let live.

References

Housing (Homeless Persons) Act 1977, HMSO; *Code of Guidance*, HMSO,
1983.
Andrew Arden, *The Homeless Persons Act*, Legal Action Group, 1983,
28A Highgate Road, London NW5 1NS, phone (01) 485 1189, (covers cases
up to September 1982).
Cambridge City Council v Persons Unknown, Queen's Bench Division of
High Court 1979-C-3146, 29 May 1979.
R v Hammersmith and Fulham London Borough Council *ex parte* Duro
Rama, 1981, *Local Government Reports* 702.
R v Salford City Council *ex parte* Devonport, High Court, *The Times*,
5 March 1983.
Pam Gallagher 'Gypsies and Housing Policy' 1980, available from Bill
Forrester.
P. Hoath 'Allocating Housing in the 1980's', *Local Government Chronicle*,
1 August 1980.
Jeremy Sandford, *Gypsies*, Abacus, 1973.
Roof, bi-monthly journal of Shelter, National Campaign for the Homeless,
from 157 Waterloo Road, London SE1, phone (01) 633 9377.

10. Health services and attitudes to health care

Although many Travellers use health services, other, often more traditional, families remain sceptical about them. Travellers traditionally look after their own, and there is distrust about such matters as immunisation. I will never forget, at a conference near Edinburgh in 1980, hearing a Scottish Traveller woman speak out passionately against the idea of any 'Gorgio' (non-Traveller) sticking needles into any of 'her people'. The distrust that has grown up over the generations can run very deep.

Hospitals

Many Travellers who move on, or are moved on, regularly will go to hospital casualty wings. While there is nothing wrong with this, it often isn't the best way of dealing with a problem. To begin with, hospital casualty departments are designed to deal with accident and emergency cases. Someone with a minor pain, or other very minor injury, may have to wait for a very long time to be fully dealt with, if there are major accidents or emergencies to be attended to. An appointment with a family doctor could get over such a problem.

Secondly, many casualty departments have been closed down ('rationalised') during the past few years, so that the distance that Travellers may have to travel to one may be enormous.

General practitioners

The GP or family doctor is the best first port of call for Travellers who plan to stop in an area for any time. As well as for serious accidents and other emergencies, the GP is the best person for day-to-day health problems.

The GP or receptionist will require that a card be filled in, if someone is registering with a doctor for the first time.Travellers who already have a medical card, should take it to the doctor's surgery. It's wise to be quite honest about how long you are planning to stay in a new doctor's area, for people registered with another doctor, planning to stay less than three months, who will then go back to that other doctor's area, should be treated as temporary patients.

Not all doctors and their receptionists give a warm welcome to Travellers. They may be overworked, may resent the mud on the carpet, or the difficult administration of people who travel around the country changing doctors as they go. But Travellers shouldn't be put off by this. Those planning to stay for some time in an area, for whom no local Traveller can recommend a kindly doctor, should ask for help at the main local post office. Or, it's possible to ask the post office for the address of the Family Practitioner Committee, which operates the National Health Services (General Medical and Pharmaceutical Services) Regulations 1974. Regulation 16(1) requires a group called the Joint Allocation Committee to find anyone not on the list of any doctor a GP, if they have either been refused acceptance by a doctor for inclusion on his list, or have been refused acceptance by a doctor as a 'temporary resident'. Regulation 21(1) says that a 'temporary resident' is

> A person requiring treatment who
> (a) is residing temporarily in a district, and is not on the list of a
>   doctor providing general medical services *in that district,* or
> (b) is moving from place to place and is not for the time being
>   resident in any place [my italics]

Many Travellers will therefore be 'temporary residents'. It is worth noting two things. One is that a doctor could be reluctant to take on a Traveller family for fear that they would make large demands on his time. However, a Wiltshire GP in early 1980 had 3,300 patients, including 200 Travellers, and said that he had 3.4 visits per year on average from Travellers, compared with 3.75 per year from others on his list.

The second point to note is that even if you are refused by a GP as a temporary or registered patient, you can ask that same doctor to provide any treatment that he decides is immediately necessary.

Other health workers

In practice, Travellers may have more contact with health visitors and midwives than doctors. These may make contact through a scheme under the auspices of the Save the Children Fund, for example, or through some social worker contact with the family in which the health visitor becomes involved. Or health visitors may initiate their own contact with a group of Travellers through an immunisation scheme of their own. In other cases, contact may be made via teachers at a school Traveller children are attending.

During the last five years or so, the health issue has become much more important, both for Travellers and for those concerned about their welfare. Three London health districts jointly fund a full-time highly qualified and experienced health worker to work solely with Traveller families. A number of eye-opening articles has appeared in the health press, and are listed at the end of this chapter.

Charges

Although there are no charges for registering with a doctor, or receiving treatment under the NHS, nor any requirements for National Insurance contributions, other costs (including glasses, dental treatment and prescriptions, to name only three) have risen steeply since 1979. Those on social security of one sort or another, children and pensioners and the chronically ill are often exempt. The local post office or social security office can supply the latest leaflets from the Department of Health and Social Security, and help in reading and understanding them. Some local authorities also have welfare benefits officers, usually attached to social services departments. The Citizen's Advice Bureau is another alternative for guidance, and its whereabouts can be checked at the post office.

Complaints

Parliament has appointed a Health Service Commissioner, originally with a staff of thirty, to investigate complaints that are brought to his attention by individual members of the public, voluntary organisations and Community Health Councils (CHCs).

If you have a complaint about Health Services, it is best to approach the nearest CHC, which can be found from the phone book or a post office, and ask them to take it up. Alternatively, a leaflet on the procedure is available from the National Association for Mental Health (MIND) at 22 Harley Street, London W1N 2ED, phone (01) 637 0741.

References

National Health Services (General Medical and Pharmaceutical Services) Regulations 1974, HMSO.
Health Services Act 1980, HMSO.

Department of Health and Social Security Circular HRC (74)5 on child health services, including school health services, HMSO, from DHSS, Alexander Fleming House, Elephant and Castle, London SE1 6BY.

Parliamentary Commissioner for Administration and Health Service, Church House, Great Smith St, London SW1P 3BW.

Kit Sampson and Dick Stockford, *Gypsy Children and their Health Needs,* Save the Children Fund, 1979. Obtainable from Mary Datchelor House, 17 Grove Lane, Camberwell, London SE5 8RD, phone (01) 703 5400.

Jocelyn Cornwell, *Improving Health Car for Travellers,* The King's Fund, 1984. Obtainable from the Fund at 126 Albert Street, London NW1 7NF.

Report, Travelling People Review Body (Irish Republic), February 1983.

11. Social security

The law and practice of social security and welfare benefits is a huge subject, and this chapter aims to cover just some of the main points, where Travellers may be treated differently from other people, or using a special procedure.

Supplementary benefits

With the difficulty at present in finding work, increasing numbers of Travellers are claiming Supplementary Benefit. A fixed address is not required, although changes of address can delay payments, particularly if you are also changing social security offices, or the post office where you pick up your Giro each fortnight. Social security is claimed either by going direct to the Department of Health and Social Security (DHSS) office, or it can now be done by post. Claim form B1 is available from many post offices.

I have encountered various practices with Travellers. One is the 'presumption of work' when fruit-picking is at its height in rural areas. There is no doubt that some Travellers work and claim benefits at the same time, risking prosecution themselves, and doing no favours to other Travellers. But that is not a good reason for refusing benefits to others who are not working. If a Traveller is not working at all, he or she should not be put off by the social security office saying that 'there is work around'.

Another practice, used in similar cases, is getting Travellers to sign away their rights to benefit for several months, and this should definitely be resisted. Of course, if someone is fiddling the system, he should be prosecuted. It is worth remembering, however, that present social security policy is to save money, firstly by not prosecuting and secondly by preventing people from claiming.

Housing benefit

If you have to pay for your accommodation, then you get housing benefit which is organised by the local council's housing department. This will obviously apply most to Travellers on proper sites, where they are paying rent.

Child benefit

The usual practice with this is that it is paid at the end of each three months to those with no fixed address. Some Travellers get around this problem by using a relative's address, in a house or on a site. There is nothing illegal about the DHSS paying it out at the end of every three months, but it does make budgeting difficult for many mothers. If at all possible, ask for a payment book, even if you have to travel some distance every few weeks to cash the benefits. Don't forget you can cash the benefits, getting up to twelve weeks at a time.

References

The Child Benefit (Claims and Payments) Regulations SI 1976 No. 964 (Supplement No. 38), authorising payment of Child Benefits to those with no fixed address at the end of every three months, HMSO.

Department of Health and Social Security, Alexander Fleming House, Elephant and Castle, London SE1 6BY, phone (01) 407 5522.
Social Security Advisory Committee, New Court, Carey House, London WC2, phone (01) 831 6111.

I Want to Appeal, from National Association of Citizens Advice Bureaux, 110 Drury Lane, London WC2, phone (01) 836 9231.
National Welfare Benefits Handbook, and other publications, from Child Poverty Action Group, 1 Macklin St, Drury Lane, London WC2B 5NH, phone (01) 405 5942.

There are numbers of legal textbooks on social security, for those who need to pursue the subject in more detail, but the best of them are expensive and any material on social security needs constant updating.

12. The police

Police practices vary from place to place, and different police forces have different ways of dealing with Travellers. Individual police officers may also sometimes step out of line. I have seen members of police forces behave with great restraint towards Travellers who were lucky not to be arrested, but I have also seen police officers behave high-handedly and make a situation such as an eviction much worse.

Private land and public land

The police should never be involved in the physical removal of Travellers from private or public land: the correct police role is to be present at any eviction to prevent any breach of the peace. The police may also arrest for any other specific offence that carries a 'power of arrest', but no police officer should actually be involved in an eviction. If they are, Travellers should take the number on their shoulders and report them to their chief constable. If you are arrested in such a case, and charged with 'obstructing' or 'assaulting' a police officer 'in the execution of his duty', then it's essential to get legal advice before you decide to plead guilty. It may be that the officer was not 'in the execution of his duty' and therefore you cannot be found guilty of either of these offences.

Harassment

Travellers do tend to get visited by the police more often than many other people. Some police officers take a hard line on matters such as vehicle offences; certainly threats of prosecution for minor offences are a significant reason for much Traveller movement. But many offences go unprosecuted if Travellers stand firm. Any Traveller who drives while disqualified, without insurance or lacking a licence, tax disc or other requirements takes a risk and only has himself to blame, if prosecuted. But such offences should not be dealt with by moving people on: that does not help those who could later be knocked down, perhaps, by an uninsured driver.

The police complaints procedure leaves a lot to be desired, and has rarely, if ever, got to grips with police malpractice towards Travellers. But it is always worth complaining about wrong or unjustified behaviour by the police, if only to challenge those who would say that no complaint means there is nothing to complain about.

Two recent cases I have come across involved sizeable searches: in one, there were 162 caravans in one town; in the other, 32 caravans on one road. The police concerned have revealed that some caravans were searched, with warrants, without any suspicion being held against the occupants of the caravans, and a large amount of property was taken, but no charges were brought. The searches related to burglaries in the surrounding area, but none of those searched were apparently told of this.

I know of no complaints against police by Travellers. One epileptic single mother tried to complain at the police station that her caravan had been ransacked and items not replaced, a story that seems to be corroborated by a passer-by who telephoned the local paper who duly printed the story. The woman was apparently referred to the area social services office.

Reference

Hughie Smith, *Police and Gypsies*, Police and Society Research Centre, July 1982, from the National Gypsy Council, Greengate St, Oldham, Greater Manchester, phone (061) 665 1924.

13. Discrimination

The questions that arise are: Are any or all Travellers protected against discrimination? In particular, are they protected by the Race Relations Act? What sort of discrimination would this include, if they are protected? What can, and should, they do if they think they have suffered discrimination?

The answer to the first of the above two questions is legally undecided. If the answer to them were 'yes', then the next two would be relatively easy to answer.

As far as protection under the Race Relations Act 1976 is concerned, our starting-point must be its Section 3. This defines the 'racial grounds' on which discrimination may take place, as well as the 'racial group' which is suffering discrimination. 'Racial grounds' means 'colour, race, nationality or ethnic or national origins'. 'Racial group' means a group of persons defined by reference to colour, race, nationality or ethnic or national origins'. Subsection 2 of section 3 says that two or more distinct racial groups can form one, and still be covered by the Act.

It would seem fairly clear that most Travellers could only be covered by the term 'ethnic', unless they could establish individual membership of a 'race'. The exception would probably be Irish Travellers, who could argue separate national origin, as indeed might Scots or Welsh Travellers.

The term 'ethnic' in section 3 of the 1976 Act has recently been defined by the House of Lords in the important case of Mandla and Another v Dowell Lee and Another. It is worth quoting a section of the headnote to that case:

> The term 'ethnic' in section 3 of the 1976 Act was to be construed relatively widely in a broad cultural and historic sense. For a group to constitute an 'ethnic group' for the purposes of the 1976 Act it had to regard itself, and be regarded by others, as a distinct community by virtue of certain characteristics, two of which were

essential. First it had to have a long shared history, of which the group was conscious of distinguishing it from other groups, and the memory of which it kept alive, and second it had to have a cultural tradition of its own, including family and social customs and manners, often but not necessarily associated with religious observance. In addition, the following characteristics could also be relevant, namely (a) either a common geographical origin or descent from a small number of common ancestors (b) a common language, which did not necessarily have to be peculiar to the group (c) a common literature peculiar to the group (d) a common religion . . . (e) the characteristic of being a minority or being an oppressed or a dominant group within a larger community.

Romany Gypsies would seem to fall clearly within the above definition, satisfying the first two requirements and then (e), probably (b) for those speaking Romany or another similar language, and possibly one or more of the others. Other Travellers may or may not fall within the definition.

It is also worth looking at the definition of Gypsy (gypsy) itself, which has also been dealt with in Chapter 1. The last significant court case which dealt with the definition was Mills v Cooper in 1967, as already mentioned. This High Court case was decided two years after the first Race Relations Act (1965) and one year before the Caravan Sites Act 1968, and was defining 'Gypsies' under the Highways Act 1959. Section 127 (c) of that Act, which is no longer law in that form, made it an offence for a person 'being a gypsy' to 'encamp on the highway'. The High Court decided that:

1. a 'gypsy' was a person 'leading a nomadic way of life with no fixed employment and no fixed abode' and
2. that a person could be a 'gypsy' one day, but not the next

Looking at this case in the light of a discussion of discrimination, it is fascinating to note:

1. That part of the Judges' reasoning was that they must presume that Parliament would not have passed discriminatory laws
2. That they made no specific reference to the Race Relations Act 1965, but seem (from 1) to have been aware of it
3. That Cripps, in his 1976 Report, at paragraph 5.16, described Section 127(c) as 'discriminatory'
4. That the world 'gypsy' was removed from the section by the

Local Government Act 1980, just after it had become Section
150 of the Highways Act 1980

All those points might weaken the case's authority in any future
legal case, and it also seems to conflict with the legal advice given to
the Race Relations Board at the time, which I will deal with shortly.

The Mills v Cooper definition of 'gypsy' was adopted, almost
word for word, by the legislators in the Caravan Sites Act 1968.
There is no doubt that the duty for certain local authorities to
provide accommodation for Traveller caravans is one catering for a
wide selection of people whose common feature is they are of a
'nomadic habit of life', without any other considerations. It is a
practical definition to deal with a practical accommodation problem.
There is no doubt that both Mills v Cooper and Section 16 of the
1968 Act would be mentioned in any future case to define Gypsy,
but neither of them is necessarily relevant in a case under the Race
Relations Act.

The arguments about whether Gypsies are protected by the
Race Relations Acts have increased steadily over the years, through
the life of the Race Relations Board (set up under the 1965 Act), the
Community Relations Commission (CRC, set up under the 1968
Act) and the Commission for Racial Equality (CRE) which currently
operates under the 1976 Act.

In 1967-8, the Race Relations Board Report said, at para 22:

> The Board has been advised that gypsies should, in general, be
> regarded as being within the terms of the Race Relations Act [i.e.
> the 1965 one]

The 1967-8 Report went on to mention action taken against licensees
of public-houses who refused to serve gypsies (unlawful discrimination 'provided there are no other reasonable grounds for
objection'), and attempts to get 'No Gypsies' signs taken down.
These were not unlawful in themselves under the 1965 Act (but now
are, under Section 29 of the 1976 Act); the Board commented,
however, that they might be if a Gypsy were deterred by such a sign
from seeking service. They also reflect the attitude of the licensee,
of course.

The extract from the 1967-8 report is highly important, because
it was quoted by a Minister while the Race Relations Bill 1976 was

being discussed. In Standing Committee 'A', on 4 May 1976, at Column 107 in the Committee *Hansard* Report, the Minister quoted as evidence that Gypsies had always been covered, so this statement would be a reason for Parliament not providing extra protection for Gypsies under special legislation. If they were to be 'found' by an important court not to have been protected by the existing Race Relations Act, the law would then need to be improved so that they were.

The Commission for Racial Equality categorises discrimination by its nature, rather than by racial group. Unlike the Commissioner for Local Government Administration (Local Ombudsman), who has published many fascinating reports on complaints against local authorities, the CRE has published hardly any reports on complaints involving Travellers. It also failed to take any action over the London Borough of Croydon's illegal refusal to provide schooling to a Gypsy child not living on their official site. The Education Minister had powers to act, and failed to, but the CRE could have taken action under Section 17(a) of the 1976 Act, which makes it unlawful for a local education authority to 'discriminate against a person . . . in the terms on which it offers to admit him to the establishment (i.e. school) as a pupil'. The CRE also declined to act when Wolverhampton City Council advertised for a 'Task Force' to evict itinerant caravan-dwellers, including Travellers, from its area. The National Gypsy Council complained under Section 29 of the 1976 Act that the advertisement indicated an intention to discriminate against Gypsies by Wolverhampton council. The CRE replied that, as Wolverhampton was designated under the Caravan Sites Act 1968, they would take no action.

In June 1980, however, the CRE did take action against a community council, a borough councillor and two community council members. It mounted a formal investigation under Section 48 of the 1976 Act into allegations that the community council and the others named had tried to prevent the borough council of Wrexham Maelor from allocating a council house to a particular local Gypsy family. The borough councillor was cleared by the investigation, as his argument had been that the particular council house, with its four bedrooms, was too small for a ten-child family. But the community council and two of its members were found to have discriminated in their attempts (albeit unsuccessful) to persuade the borough council not to allocate the house to the Gypsy family.

The CRE's report, at paragraphy 1.2, stated quite clearly:

We take the view that Gypsies in the UK, who number about 50,000, constitute an ethnic minority group and as such are protected against discrimination under the Race Relations Act 1976.

And they went on to say, at paragraph 1.4:

> Persons who oppose gypsies taking up residence in their neighbourhood should be aware that they are contravening the Race Relations Act if they attempt to induce a housing authority or landlord to withhold accommodation or land from Gypsy families. This could also be true for persons who oppose proposals by local authorities to establish gypsy caravan sites, and this includes public representatives such as local Councils or individual Councillors, whether or not they are acting at the behest of their electors. Authorities or landlords who submit to such pressure would, of course, also be in breach of the law. We hope that the publication of this report will promote a better understanding of the law in this area and show that the Commission is determined to enforce it.

It is important to remember that the CRE's report on the community council case does not have the same legal status as a court decision. The National Gypsy Council's 1983 Report quotes a letter from the office of the Director of Public Prosecutions to the Commission for Racial Equality, concluding that the word Gypsy 'might be understood in either that sense [racial group] or more generally as meaning nomads, [but] it seems unlikely . . . that we would obtain convictions [under the Race Relations Act]'. This in fact means that prosecutions for 'incitement to racial hatred' under the Public Order Act (amended by the Race Relations Acts) might not be brought through fear of losing them.

Against that calculation must now be set the important 1983 House of Lords case of Mandla v Lee. This was the case which decided that Sikhs were an 'ethnic group' whose children were entitled to wear their turbans in school. The House of Lords, in overturning the Court of Appeal decision by Lord Denning and others, decided that there were certain indicators of an 'ethnic group', including a common geographical origin, common culture, common language and common religion. The belief of people that they belonged to such an ethnic group was also important (compare the importance of recognition by a group of Gypsies as proving someone's identity as a Gypsy as a social fact, covered in Chapter 1). There seems little doubt that Gypsies would satisfy the House of Lords' test on common culture, common language and belief in belonging to a very distinct social group, and possibly also in some cases common religion. There is nothing to prevent the Traveller community being assessed as including more than one ethnic group, and it certainly seems clear that Gypsies, as a whole, satisfy the House of Lords criteria.

If this is the case, then Gypsies would not only be protected against 'direct discrimination', refusal of service in pubs, shops and in many other instances merely because they were Gypsies, but would also be protected against 'indirect discrimination' where a 'requirement' or 'condition' is applied to something which makes it highly unlikely that the Gypsy could comply. The exact detail of this is in Section 1 of the Race Relations Act 1976.

Discrimination occurs all the time against Travellers, and the Race Relations Act 1976 is a largely unexplored tool for change, even if it will not immediately bring about that change in attitudes which would make the Act unnecessary. Of all known efforts that are made to prevent Traveller caravan sites being set up, only one director of the firm CTI Developments in Wales has been taken to task for trying to persuade the local authority not to set up a Gypsy site near him, though I know of many who have used similar pressure to stop site provision in their areas.

The Race Relations Act makes it possible for an individual to take a company, club or whatever to a civil court, usually a County Court, over discrimination they may have suffered. Advisers of Travellers should not be slow to realise that is an avenue to be used, and should mention it, together with the adverse publicity which could result, when dealing with someone who is discriminating.

Another example of discrimination is in housing. Housing departments, as mentioned, have to operate rules for admission to housing lists, and these may indirectly work against Travellers who move between districts, either voluntarily or because they are pushed on, because they do not have the continuous residence required. Mortgages are another area of concern. The Nationwide Building Society (quoted in D. Sibley, J. Roscoe and P. Scraton (eds) *Towards Enforced Assimilation,* Gypsy and Traveller Education Council, 1974, but now out of print) said in 1973 that 'while (we) don't discriminate against Gypsies, any nomad applying would need to produce three years of receipts of trading before even being con-

sidered'. I myself got a bank mortgage in 1982 solely on the strength
of my then salary, which perhaps stood more chance of coming to an
end than many Traveller businesses.

Further examples of discrimination are legion. A working men's
club in Kent in 1977 put up a notice which said 'No Gypsies,
Didicois or Mumpers allowed in'. After a complaint, the notice was
removed, but the club would then only serve the 'flash' Gypsies,
refusing service to the others. One young Traveller applied for the
renewal of his membership card (which entitles the holder to use
any other similar club in the country) and was refused by someone
saying 'we don't want you' and 'you're too young, anyway'. The
man is married and over eighteen, and the club is the only place to
socialise in that town.

But the worst example of discrimination I have met would only
have marginally fallen within the provisions of the Race Relations
Act. A family was rehoused from a leaky tent in which its members
had lived since their caravan burnt out. They moved into a council
house, and their neighbour immediately wrote to the district council,
protesting and asking for their removal. (This could, of course, have
been dealt with under the 1976 Act.) The neighbours then organised
a petition against the family, because they did not 'integrate into the
community'. Fortunately, the petition was never pursued. The
eldest son of the family went to school, effectively for the first time,
at thirteen. He complained of intimidation on the bus on the way,
and his bullying while at school was witnessed by another pupil who
burst into tears while telling me of it. The Traveller boy truanted
from school, but the area education office did not know what action
it was best to take. In the midst of debate, the family vanished from
the council house, and never returned.

Action

It is well worthwhile using the 1976 Act. The CRE can support
certain cases financially, and booklets giving advice are widely
available.

Public Sector Education complaints must first go to the Education Minister, but schools who reject Travellers should be challenged, subtly and diplomatically at first, then by legal action, even
if, in the end, it will not be possible for particular Traveller children
to go there, because of the school staff's attitude.

Housing and other public services need to be tackled on their method of dealing with Travellers, and the Act provides the opportunity to do so.

In cases of Licensed premises, another method is possible. All licensees have to renew their licenses, with magistrates dealing with alcohol license applications or renewals. The hearings are sometimes called 'brewster sessions' and in London are held every quarter. Applicants must appear in person, and prove that they are fit and proper people, in character, health and temperament, to hold a licence.

Anyone may object. If Travellers have been refused service for no good reason, they should be encouraged to object. Further, a letter to the brewery, or its area manager, with perhaps a complaint also to the CRE, to bring the whole matter into the open, will perhaps embarrass the licensee sufficiently for him to change his attitude.

Dry note

A publican in Wisbech, Cambridgeshire, put up a sign saying 'No Travellers served' and then found all his commercial traveller customers had disappeared, as well as the Gypsies he was trying to keep out!

References

Race Relations Act 1976, HMSO, Commission for Racial Equality, Elliott House, 10/12 Allington St, London SW1, phone (01) 828 7022.

Report of Four Formal Investigations into Alleged Pressure to Discriminate by (i) Brymbo Community Council (ii) Councillor K. Rogers (iii) Mrs I. Stapley (iv) Mrs B. Greenaway, available from CRE.

Mandla and Another v Dowell Lee and Another, House of Lords, 1983 (1), *All England Law Reports* 1062.

Report on Discrimination, National Gypsy Council 1982, from Greengate St, Oldham, Greater Manchester, phone (061) 665 1924.

Appendix A

Select list of general reading materials and useful organisations

General reading

Don Kennington, *Gypsies and Travelling People*, October 1982, from Capital Planning Information, 6 Castle St, Edinburgh EH2 3AT (£5). (Don Kennington previously compiled Bibliography No. 79 in February 1977 for the Greater London Council Research Library.)
Martin Smith, *Gypsies: Where Now?* Young Fabian Pamphlet 42, 1975 from Fabian society, 11 Dartmouth St, London SW1H 9BN, phone (01) 222 8877.

Accommodation for Gypsies; Gypsy Legislation and Proposals; Gypsy Matters, reports of three public meetings, 1978, 1979 and 1980, Land Institute, 93 High St, Epsom, Surrey.
Urban Wasteland: Report on dormant land, Civic Trust, October 1977, from 17 Carlton House Terrace, London SW1Y 5AW, phone (01) 930 0914.

Government publications

Caravans Sites and Control of Development Act 1960; Caravan Sites Act 1968; Ministry of Housing and Local Government Circulars 6/62, 26/66, 60/67; MHLG Circular 49/68; Department of the Environment Circulars 38/70; DoE Circular 28/77 (repealed all previous ones), 57/78, 11/79, 8/81; Home Office Circular 8/81.
Accommodation for Gypsies, the Cripps Report, 1977.
Smith and Gmelches, *The Accommodation Needs of Long-distance and Regional Travellers*, (obtainable at DoE Library, Marsham St, London SW1).

Organisations

National Gypsy Council, Greengate St, Oldham, Greater Manchester, phone (061) 665 1924: annual reports plus reports on education, discrimination, quality of site provision, Wales, London boroughs.
The Romany Guild, 50-6 Temple Mills Lane, Stratford, London E15, phone (01) 555 7214: various reports, including *East London Gypsies*.
Save the Children Fund, Mary Datchelor House, 17 Grove Lane, Camberwell, London SE5 8RD, phone (01) 703 5400.

Scotland
Hugh Gentleman and Susan Swift, *Scotland's Travelling People*, Scottish Development Department, HMSO, 1971.
Scotland's Travelling People, three reports of the Secretary of State's Advisory Committee, 1971-4, 1975-8, 1979-82, HMSO.

Northern Ireland
Services for Travelling People in Northern Ireland, review by the Co-ordinating Committee on Social Problems, July 1981.

Southern Ireland
Report of the Travelling People Review Body, Dublin Stationery Office, February 1983, from Government Publications Sales Office, Sun Alliance House, Molesworth St, Dublin 2.

Western Europe
Marthe Bilmans, *The Legal Position of Gypsies in Western Europe*, Interim Report to the Romano Kongreso, Geneva, April-August 1978.

Her Majesty's Stationery Offices, from which government publications can be obtained, are at:
49 High Holborn, London WC1V 6HB, phone (01) 583 9876 or (01) 928 6977;
13a Castle St, Edinburgh EH2 3AR;
Brazenose St, Manchester, M60 8AS;
Southern House, Wine St, Bristol BS1 2BQ;
258 Broad St, Birmingham B1 2HE;
80 Chichester St, Belfast BT1 4JY.

Appendix B

Caravan Sites Act 1968 (as amended by Town and Country Planning Act 1971, Local Government Act 1972, Local Government Planning and Land Act 1980 and Criminal Justice Act 1982)

GIPSY ENCAMPMENTS
Provision of sites by local authorities

Duty of local authorities to provide sites for gipsies.

6.—(1) Subject to the provisions of this and the next following section, it shall be the duty of every local authority being the council of a county or London borough to exercise their powers under Section 24 of the Caravan Sites and Control of Development Act 1960 (provision of caravan sites) so far as may be necessary to provide adequate accommodation for gipsies residing in or resorting to their area.

(2) The council of a Metropolitan county or London borough shall not in any case be required under subsection (1) of this section to provide accommodation for more than fifteen caravans at a time in each district in the county or, as the case may be, in the London borough.

(3) Any local authority may defray or contribute towards expenditure incurred or to be incurred under this Part of this Act by any other authority.

(4) The powers of a local authority under the said section 24 shall include power to provide, in or in connection with sites for the accommodation of gipsies, working space and facilities for the carrying on of such activities as are normally carried on by them; but subsection (1) of this section shall not apply to the powers conferred by this subsection.

Functions of district councils.

7.(1) The duty imposed by section 6(1) of this Act on the council of a county shall extend only to be determining what sites are to be provided and acquiring or appropriating the necessary land; and it shall be the duty of the council of the district in which any such site is located to exercise all other powers under section 24 of the Caravan Sites and Control of Development Act 1960 in relation to the site.

(2) The charges to be made by the council of a county district pursuant to subsection 3 of the said section 24 in respect of any such site shall be such as may be determined by the council of the county; and the council of the county shall pay to the council of the district sums equal to their expenditure reasonably incurred under this section (including the proper proportion of the remuneration and expenses of their officers and other administrative expenditure) so far as it exceeds their receipts thereunder.

(3) The council of any county district may, with the approval of the council of the county concerned, agree with the council of any other such district for the discharge by one of those councils, as agent for the other, of such of the functions under this section of the latter council as may be specified in the agreement.

8.—(1) Before adopting a proposal to acquire or appropriate land for a site pursuant to this Part of the Act, the council of a county shall consult the council of the county district in which the land is situated and such other authorities and persons as they consider appropriate.

(2) If objection is made to any such proposal by the council of a county district in or adjacent to which the land is situated and is not disposed of in consultation with the council of the county, the council of the county district may give notice of the objection to the Minister.

(3) After considering any such objection the Minister may, as appears to him proper, give directions to the council of the county —

    (*a*) to abandon the proposal

    (*b*) to proceed with the proposal

    (*c*) to make an application for planning permission in respect of the proposed use of the land;

and any application for planning permission made pursuant to such directions shall be deemed to be referred to the Minister under section 35 of the Town and Country Planning Act 1971.

9.— The Secretary of State may, if at any time it appears to him to be necessary to do so, give directions to any local authority to which subsection (1) of section 6 of this Act applies requiring them to provide, pursuant to that section, such sites or additional sites, for the accommodation of such numbers of caravans, as may be specified in the directions; and any such directions shall be enforceable, on the application of the Secretary of State, by mandamus.

Control of unauthorised encampments

Prohibition of unauthorised camping in designated areas.

10.—(1) In any area designated under the following provisions of this Act as an area to which this section applies it shall be an offence for any person being a gipsy to station a caravan for the purpose of residing for any period —

> (*a*) on any land situated within the boundaries of a highway; or
>
> (*b*) on any other unoccupied land; or
>
> (*c*) on any occupied land without the consent of the occupier.

(2) In proceedings against any person for an offence under this section it shall be a defence to prove that the caravan was stationed on the land in consequence of illness, mechanical breakdown or other immediate emergency and that he removed it (or intended to remove it) as soon as reasonably practicable.

(3) A person guilty of an offence under this section shall be liable on summary conviction to a fine not exceeding £25 and if the offence of which he is convicted is continued after the conviction he shall be guilty of a further offence and shall be liable in respect thereof to a fine not exceeding £5 for every day on which the offence is so continued.

Orders for removal of unlawfully parked caravans and their occupants.

11.—(1) In any area to which section 10 of this Act applies, a magistrates' court may, on a complaint made by a local authority, and if satisfied that a caravan is stationed on land within that Authority's area in contravention of that section, make an order requiring any caravan (whether or not identified in the order) which is so stationed on the land to be removed together with any person residing in it.

(2) An order under this section may authorise the local authority to take such steps as are reasonably necessary to ensure that the order is complied with and in particular, may authorise the authority, by its officers and servants —

> (*a*) to enter upon the land specified in the order; and
>
> (*b*) to take, in relation to any caravan to be removed pursuant to the order, such steps for securing entry and rendering it suitable for removal as may be so specified.

(3) The local authority shall not enter upon any occupied land unless they have given to the owner and occupier at least 24 hours notice of their intention to do so, or unless after reasonable inquiries they are unable to ascertain their names and addresses.

(4) A person who intentionally obstructs any person acting in the exercise of any power conferred on him by an order under this section shall be guilty of an offence and liable on summary conviction to a fine not exceeding £200.

(5) A constable in uniform may arrest without warrant anyone whom he reasonbly suspects to be guilty of an offence under this section.

(6) Where a complaint is made under this section, a summons issued by the court requiring the person or persons to whom it is directed to appear before the court to answer to the complaint may be directed —
    (*a*) to the occupant of a particular caravan stationed on the land in question; or
    (*b*) to all occupants of caravans stationed there, without naming him or them.

(7) Where it is impracticable to serve such a summons on a person named in it, it shall be treated as duly served on him if a copy of it is fixed in a prominent place to the caravan concerned; and where such a summons is directed to the unnamed occupants of caravans, it shall be treated as duly served on those occupants if a copy of it is fixed in a prominent place to every caravan stationed on the land in question at the time when service is thus effected.

(8) The local authority shall take such steps as may be reasonably practicable to secure that a copy of such summons is displayed on the land in question (otherwise than by being fixed to a caravan) in a manner designed to ensure that it is likely to be seen by any person camping on the land.

(9) Notice of any such summons shall be given by the local authority to the owner of the land in question and to any occupier of that land unless, after reasonable inquiries, the authority is unable to ascertain the name and address of the owner or occupier; and the owner of any such land and any occupier of any such land shall be entitled to appear and to be heard in the proceedings.

(10) Section 55(2) of the Magistrates' Court Act 1980 (warrant for arrest of defendant failing to appear) does not apply to proceedings on a complaint made under this section.

12.—(1) Subject to subsection (3) below, the Minister may by order made on the application of a county council or London borough council designate the area of that council as an area to which section 10 of this Act applies.

(2) Subject to subsection (3) below, the Minister may by order made on the joint application of a county council and one or more councils of districts within that county designate the area of the district or, as the case may be, the combined areas of the districts, as an area to which section 10 of this Act applies.

(3) The Minister shall not make an order under subsection (1) or (2) above in respect of any area unless it appears to him either that adequate provision is made in the area for the accommodation of gipsies residing in or resorting to the area, or that in all the circumstances it is not necessary or expedient to make any such provision.

(4) An order under this section may be revoked by an order made by the Minister, either on the application of the authority or authorities which made the original application or without such an application.

(5) The power of the Minister to make orders under this section shall be exercisable by statutory instrument; and any statutory instrument made by virtue of this section shall be subject to annulment in pursuance of a resolution of either House of Parliament.

(6) Where an order under this section is made in respect of any area it shall be the duty of the county council for that area or, as the case may be, the London borough council concerned to take such steps as are reasonably practicable to inform gipsies within the area of the making and effect of the order.

(2) Where by virtue of the Local Government Act 1972 (which, among other things, reorganised local authority areas) a designation made before 1st April 1974 under section 12 of the 1968 Act as originally enacted (and not revoked) relates to part only of the area of a county, any order which is made on the application of the council of that county under subsection (1) or (2) of the section substituted for section 12 of the 1968 Act by subsection (1) above shall be made to extend only to an area which does not include the area designated before 1st April 1974.

Twin-unit
caravans.

13.—(1) A structure designed or adapted for human habitation which —

    (*a*) is composed of not more than two sections separately constructed and designed to be assembled on a site by means of bolts, clamps or other devices; and

    (*b*) is, when assembled, physically capable of being moved by road from one place to another (whether by being towed, or by being transported on a motor vehicle or trailer),

shall not be treated as not being (or as not having been) a caravan within the meaning of Part I of the Caravan Sites and Control of Development Act 1960 by reason only that it cannot lawfully be so moved on a highway when assembled.

(2) For the purposes of Part I of the Caravan Sites and Control of Development Act 1960, the expression "caravan" shall not include a structure designed or adapted for human habitation which falls within paragraphs (*a*) and (*b*) of the foregoing subsection if its dimensions when assembled exceed any of the following limits, namely —

    (*a*) length (exclusive of any drawbar): 60 feet (18.288 metres);

    (*b*) width: 20 feet (6.096 metres);

    (*c*) overall height of living accommodation (measured internally from the floor at the lowest to the ceiling at the highest level): 10 feet (3.048 metres).

(3) The Minister may by order made by statutory instrument after consultation with such persons or bodies as appear to him to be concerned substitute for any figure mentioned in subsection (2) of this section such other figure as may be specified in the order.

(4) Any statutory instrument made by virtue of subsection (3) of this section shall be subject to annulment in pursuance of a resolution of either House of Parliament.

Offences.

14.—(1) Where an offence under this Act committed by a body corporate is proved to have been committed with the consent or connivance of or to be attributable to any neglect on the part of, any director, manager, secretary or other similar officer of the body corporate or any person who is purporting to act in any such capacity, he as well as the body corporate shall be guilty of that offence and shall be liable to be proceeded against and punished accordingly.

(2) Proceedings for an offence under this Act may be instituted by any local authority.

15.— There shall be defrayed out of moneys provided by Parliament any increase which may arise in consequence of this Act in the sums payable out of moneys so provided in respect of rate support grant under the Local Government Act 1966.

16.— In this Act the following expressions have the following meanings that is to say —

"caravan" has the same meaning as in Part I of the Caravan Sites and Control of Development Act 1960, as amended by this Act;

"gipsies" means persons of nomadic habit of life, whatever their race or origin, but does not include members of an organised group of travelling showmen, or of persons engaged in travelling circuses, travelling together as such;

"local authority" has the same meaning as in section 24 of the Caravan Sites and Control of Development Act 1960;

"the Minister" means, in England other than Monmouthshire, the Secretary of State and in Wales and Monmouthshire the Secretary of State;

"planning permission" means permission under Part III of the Town and Country Planning Act 1971.

17.—(1) This Act may be cited as the Caravan Sites Act 1968.

(2) This Act, except Part II, shall come into force at the expiration of the period of one month beginning with the day on which it is passed, and Part II shall come into force on such date as the Minister may by order made by statutory instrument appoint.

(3) This Act does not extend to Scotland or Northern Ireland.

CARAVAN SITES AND CONTROL OF
DEVELOPMENT ACT 1960
Provision of caravan sites by local authorities

24.—(1) A local authority shall have power within their area to provide sites where caravans may be brought, whether for holidays or other temporary purposes or for use as permanent residences, and to manage the sites or lease them to some other person.

(2) Subject to the provisions of this section, a local authority shall have power to do anything appearing to them desirable in connection with the provision of such sites, and in particular —

(*a*) to acquire land which is in use as a caravan site, or which has been laid out as a caravan site, or

(*b*) to provide for the use of those occupying caravan sites any services or facilities for their health or convenience; and in exercising their powers under this section the local authority shall have regard to any standards which may have been specified by the Minister under subsection (6) of section five of this Act.

(3) The local authority shall make in respect of the use of sites managed by them, and of any services or facilities provided or made available under this section, such reasonable charges as they may determine.

(4) A local authority may make available the services and facilities provided under the section for those who do not normally reside in the area of the local authority as freely as for those who do.

(5) A local authority shall, in the performance of their functions under this section, have power, where it appears to them that a caravan site or an additional caravan site is needed in their area, or that land which is in use as a caravan site should in the interests of the users of caravans be taken over by the local authority, to acquire land, or any interest in land compulsorily.

(6) The power of a local authority under the last foregoing subsection to acquire land, or any interest in land, compulsorily shall be exercisable in any particular case on their being authorised to do so by the Minister, and the Acquisition of Land (Authorisation Procedure) Act, 1946, shall have effect in relation to the acquisition of land, or any interest in land, under the said subsection as if this Act had been in force, immediately before the commencement of that Act.

(7) A local authority shall not have power under this section to provide caravans.

(8) In this section the expression "local authority" includes the council of a county and a joint planning board constituted under section four of the Act of 1947 for an area which consists of or includes a National Park as defined by subsection (3) of section five of the National Parks and

Access to the Countryside Act, 1949, or any part of such a
National Park.

SCHEDULES

FIRST SCHEDULE
CASES WHERE A CARAVAN SITE LICENCE IS NOT REQUIRED

Use within curtilage of a dwellinghouse

1. A site licence shall not be required for the use of land as a
caravan site if the use is incidental to the enjoyment as such
of a dwellinghouse within the curtilage of which the land is
situated.

Use by a person travelling with a caravan for one or two nights

2. Subject to the provisions of paragraph 13 of this Schedule,
a site licence shall not be required for the use of land as a
caravan site by a person travelling with a caravan who brings
the caravan on to the land for a period which includes not
more than two nights —

    (*a*) if during that period no other caravan is stationed
for the purposes of human habitation on that land
or any adjoining land in the same occupation, and

    (*b*) if, in the period of twelve months ending with the
day on which the caravan is brought on to the land,
the number of days on which a caravan was stationed
anywhere on that land or the said adjoining land for
the purpose of human habitation did not exceed
twenty-eight.

Use of holding of five acres or more in certain circumstances

3.—(1) Subject to the provisions of paragraph 13 of this
Schedule, a site licence shall not be required for use as a
caravan site of land which comprises, together with any
adjoining land which is in the same occupation and has not
been built on, not less than five acres —

    (*a*) if in the period of twelve months ending with the
day on which the land is used as a caravan site the
number of days on which a caravan was stationed
anywhere on that land or on the said adjoining land
for the purposes of human habitation did not exceed
twenty-eight, and

    (*b*) if in the said period of twelve months not more than
three caravans were so stationed at any one time.

(2) The Minister may by order contained in a statutory instrument provide that in any such area as may be specified in the order this paragraph shall have effect subject to the modification —

    (*a*) that for the reference in the foregoing sub-paragraph to five acres there shall be substituted a reference to such smaller acreage as may be specified in the order, or

    (*b*) that for the condition specified in head (*a*) of that sub-paragraph there shall be substituted a condition that the use in question falls between such dates in any year as may be specified in the order.

or subject to modification in both respects.

(3) The Minister may make different orders under this paragraph as respects different areas, and an order under this paragraph may be varied by a subsequent order made thereunder.

(4) An order under this paragraph shall come into force on such date as may be specified in the order, being a date not less than three months after the order is made; and the Minister shall publish notice of the order in a local newspaper circulating in the locality affected by the order and in such other ways as appear to him to be expedient for the purpose of drawing the attention of the public to the order.

Sites occupied and supervised by exempted organisations

4. Subject to the provisions of paragraph 13 of this Schedule, a site licence shall not be required for the use as a caravan site of land which is occupied by an organisation which holds for the time being a certificate of exemption granted under paragraph 12 of this Schedule (hereinafter referred to as an exempted organisation) if the use is for purposes of recreation and is under the supervision of the organisation.

Sites approved by exempted organisations

5.—(1) Subject to the provisions of paragraph 13 of this Schedule, a site licence shall not be required for the use as a caravan site of land as respects which there is in force a certificate issued under this paragraph by an exempted organisation if not more than five caravans are at the time stationed for the purposes of human habitation on the land to which the certificate relates.

(2) For the purposes of this paragraph an exempted organisation may issue as respects any land a certificate

stating that the land has been approved by the exempted organisation for use by its members for the purposes of recreation.

(3) The certificate shall be issued to the occupier of the land to which it relates, and the organisation shall send particulars to the Minister of all certificates issued by the organisation under this paragraph.

(4) A certificate issued by an exempted organisation under this paragraph shall specify the date on which it is come into force and the period for which it is to continue in force, being a period not exceeding one year.

Meetings organised by exempted organisations

6. Subject to the provisions of paragraph 13 of this Schedule, a site licence shall not be required for the use of land as a caravan site if the use is under the supervision of an exempted organisation and is in pursuance of arrangements made by that organisation for a meeting for its members lasting not more than five days.

Agricultural and forestry workers

7. Subject to the provisions of paragraph 13 this Schedule, a site licence shall not be required for the use as a caravan site of agricultural land for the accommodation during a particular season of a person or persons employed in farming operations on land in the same occupation.

8. Subject to the provisions of paragraph 13 of this Schedule, a site licence shall not be required for the use of land as a caravan site for the accommodation during a particular season of a person or persons employed on land in the same occupation, being land used for the purposes of forestry (including afforestation).

Building and engineering sites

9. Subject to the provisions of paragraph 13 of this Schedule, a site licence shall not be required for the use as a caravan site of land which forms part of, or adjoins, land on which building or engineering operations are being carried out (being operations for the carrying out of which permission under Part III of the Act of 1947 has, if required, been granted) if that use is for the accommodation of a person or persons employed in connection with the said operations.

Travelling showmen

10.—(1) Subject to the provisions of paragraph 13 of this Schedule, a site licence shall not be required for the use of land as a caravan site by a travelling showman who is a member of an organisation of travelling showmen which holds for the time being a certificate granted under this paragraph and who is, at the time, travelling for the purposes of his business or who has taken up winter quarters on the land with his equipment for some period falling between the beginning of October in any year and the end of March in the following year.

(2) For the purposes of this paragraph the Minister may grant a certificate to any organisation recognised by him as confining its membership to bona fide travelling showmen; and a certificate so granted may be withdrawn by the Minister at any time.

Sites occupied by licensing authority

11. A site licence shall not be required for the use as a caravan site of land occupied by the local authority in whose area the land is situated.

Gipsy sites occupied by county councils or regional councils

11a. A site licence shall not be required for the use of land occupied by a county council, or in Scotland by a regional council, as a caravan site providing accommodation for gipsies.

Certification of exempted organisations

12.—(1) For the purposes of paragraphs 4, 5 and 6 of this Schedule the Minister may grant a certificate of exemption to any organisation as to which he is satisfied that its objects include the encouragement or promotion of recreational activities.

(2) A certificate granted under this paragraph may be withdrawn by the Minister at any time.

Power to withdraw certain exemptions

13.—(1) The Minister may on the application of a local authority by order provide that, in relation to such land situated in their area as may be specified in the order, this Schedule shall have effect as if paragraphs 2 to 10, or such one or more of those paragraphs as may be so specified, were omitted from this Schedule.

(2) An order under this paragraph —

    (*a*) shall come into force on such date as may be specified therein, and

    (*b*) may, on the application of the local authority on whose application it was made, be varied or revoked by a subsequent order made thereunder,

and, except in the case of an order the sole effect of which is to revoke in whole or part a previous order, the local authority shall, not less then three months before the order comes into force, cause a notice setting out the effect of the order and the date on which it comes into force to be published in the London Gazette or, if the land is in Scotland, in the Edinburgh Gazette and in a local newspaper circulating in the locality in which the land to which the order relates is situated.

LOCAL GOVERNMENT PLANNING AND LAND ACT 1980
Grants for caravan sites

Grants in respect of caravan sites for gipsies.

70.—(1) This section applies to expenditure of a capital nature incurred by any local authority under section 24 of the Caravan Sites and Control of Development Act 1960 (provison of caravan sites by local authorities) in respect of caravan sites provided for the accommodation of gipsies.

(2) The Secretary of State may, with the approval of the Treasury, make out of money provided by Parliament grants in respect of expenditure which, in his opinion, is expenditure to which this section applies.

(3) Any grants under this section shall be made on such terms and conditions (if any) as the Secretary of State may, with the approval of the Treasury, determine.

(4) In this section —

"caravan" has the meaning assigned to it by the Caravan Sites and Control of Development Act 1960; and

"gipsies" has the meaning assigned to it by the Caravan Sites Act 1968.

Acts of Parliament and Regulations

Government Department Circulars

Department of Education and
    Science
1/80, 78
1/81, 72, 76
Department of the Environment
24/73, 17
28/77, 2, 21, 22
8/81, 49
23/83, 70
Home Office
8/81, 49
Ministry of Housing and local
    Government (DoE's predecessor)
    42/60, 24

Legal Cases

Index

InterChange

Based in Kentish Town, North London, InterChange is a community centre in the widest sense; providing a comprehensive range of projects, services and facilities, it exists to stimulate greater community involvement and activity.

From the InterChange Centre, we run community arts and education projects including a Weekend Arts College, an alternative school and a city farm. The multi-media resource centre gives low cost access to expensive audio-visual, printing and computing technology. InterChange's organisation development team provide advice, training and consultancy on all aspects of running community organisations.

InterChange Books are aimed at helping groups and individuals organise themselves effectively and achieve their own objectives. Drawing on InterChange's wide experience of community action, InterChange Books are practical and clearly written handbooks, which de-mystify professional topics such as the law, publishing and printing, and which help people cope with bureaucracy.